KEEP THE
Change

BECKY
Tirabassi

KEEP THE
Change

Breaking Through to
Permanent Transformation

INTEGRITY®
PUBLISHERS
Nashville

KEEP THE CHANGE

Published by Integrity Publishers, a division of Integrity Media, Inc., 5250
Virginia Way, Suite 110, Brentwood, TN 37027.

HELPING PEOPLE WORLDWIDE EXPERIENCE *the* MANIFEST PRESENCE *of* GOD.

Cover Design: David Uttley
Cover Photo: Photonica
Interior Design: Susan Browne

Library of Congress Cataloging-in-Publication Data
Tirabassi, Becky, 1954-
Keep the change : breaking through to permanent transformation / by
Becky Tirabassi.
p. cm.
ISBN 1-59145-051-9 (hardcover)
ISBN 1-59145-122-1 (international paperback)
1. Success. 2. Change (Psychology) I. Title.
BJ1611.2.T57 2003
158—dc21

2003008725

Printed in the United States of America
03 04 05 06 07 BVG 9 8 7 6 5 4 3 2 1

contents

Thank you . . .

To my husband, Roger Tirabassi, the most genuine "helper" I have ever known. His fingerprints, voice, and wise counsel are upon every page in this book. Anyone who grabs on to his wisdom will benefit from hours of free, incredibly valuable information—as I have done for more than twenty-five years.

To Trisha Hubbs. I met Trisha when she was working in the television industry. We connected in a very serendipitous way. Because she had heard me speak at a convention ten years earlier, she came to a television taping where Roger and I were guests. That day we began a friendship that has turned into a working partnership with the goal of seeing the Change Your Life message find a home on daily television and radio. She is an extremely gifted writer to whom I am eternally grateful! She has given more than hours to this book; she has been able to take my spontaneous passion and craft it into the written word.

To Byron Williamson and Joey Paul at Integrity Publishers for giving me the opportunity to write *Keep the Change*.

To my staff, Heidi Sisto and Carissa Dunn, for hours of typing when it was not convenient but necessary.

To my family and friends for sharing their stories in this book and encouraging us all to keep the change.

For More Information . . .

For more information on Change Your Life® Events, resources,
or to contact Becky, write, call, or e-mail . . .

Becky Tirabassi Change Your Life®, Inc.
Box 9672
Newport Beach, CA 92660
800-444-6189
949-644-8044 fax
letters@beckytirabassi.com
www.beckytirabassi.com

An Unusual Request

If you . . .

- ► have tried it all and believe nothing will ever work,
- ► feel you cannot face another disappointment,
- ► are paralyzed by fear of failure,
- ► find yourself resentful and needing to make unexpected, unwelcome changes in your life,
- ► have quit fighting because of cynicism (yours or others),
- ► are plagued by negative voices,
- ► are stalled by complacency,
- ► hesitate to bother trying because history tells you the ground you gain will never last,
- ► have almost given up on your dream . . .

Yet . . .

- ► in your desperate, quiet struggle for hope, you are willing to consider one more radical approach to permanent transformation . . .

then *Keep the Change* is written for you.

In fact, if you are simply seeking a reason to believe in the *possibility* of changing your life forever, you are holding the right book.

No matter where you are on your journey toward real and lasting breakthrough in any area of your life, I AM ABSOLUTELY CERTAIN EACH OF YOU CAN SUCCEED.

Some of you are strugglers. It is difficult to imagine a finish line because just surviving the day-to-day battle is consuming. You have read countless books intended to jump-start your life, but despite your best intentions you somehow always fall back to the familiar habits, places, and ruts. I am writing most passionately to you with a hope that you might finally get rid of the things that steal your potential and keep you from breaking through once and for all.

Some of you are lofty dreamers. You know in your soul that you are meant for more. But no matter how hard you push or fight, it seems you never make it past a certain point. And frankly, you are worn out and feel beat up. My motivation in writing this book is to offer you encouragement to hold on to your dreams until they are fulfilled. I want to fuel the endurance you need to reach your goals, no matter how large or small.

I am absolutely certain that no matter what you want to change, improve, or achieve in your life, you can do it. I want you to pick up and dust off those dreams, goals, and intentions one more time. You will discover that there is no escape hatch where we're heading. This time, the change and progress are irreversible.

I know your bags are heavy with past failures and unfulfilled purposes. And as you look out from this place, the path is daunting. So throughout this book, I will come alongside and show you ways to lighten the load as you go.

Because I vividly remember what and who gave me hope and courage in my pursuit to fulfill a lifelong dream, achieve many challenging goals, and overcome numerous personal struggles, I will offer you hope.

Because I still recall how many times I felt discouraged or desperate or overwhelmed or skeptical in the beginning and middle stages of the pursuit of permanent transformation, I will encourage you.

Many times I only saw the enormity of the emotional, financial, and relational difficulties ahead of me. But I experienced a renewed strength to keep my resolve, knowing there were other sojourners next to me the entire way. I AM ON THE JOURNEY WITH YOU.

Because I found rest through the comforting words of a friend or sponsor who showed compassion for my slow, lazy steps and even offered patience with my outright stumbles on the road to achievement, health, and recovery, I will be one of your accountability partners.

Just as I received incredible encouragement from seeing and hearing trailblazers—whether I knew them or not—who achieved their goals ahead of me and gave some good advice, I am committed to being a trailblazer for you.

Because I have tested this approach, I am offering it to you as a radical but practical way to bring breakthrough into your life. I hope you will find the stories I share here insightful. Whether or not you struggle with my particular challenges, such as alcoholism or anger or an unfulfilled dream, allow the stories to help you look honestly at the areas in your own life in which you wrestle for freedom.

I believe your ability to hold on to your dreams, achieve your goals, or overcome your struggles lies in the following proven yet radical approach to permanent transformation.

Define the truth about yourself by looking as honestly at yourself as you look at others. Then *keep the truth alive.*

Remember the feelings of determination or pain or shame that instigated your desire to change, and harness them. *Never forget those memories,* and let them powerfully serve to keep you both humble and resolved for your entire life.

Know your personality. You have been born with a basic operating system made up of unique strengths and weaknesses. How *you* deal with everything, including and especially change, is specific to you.

Daily, even hourly if necessary, resist negative thoughts until doing so is second nature. Fighting the battle in your mind— one thought at a time—must become a lifelong habit if you desire to experience happiness, health, balance, and success in all your endeavors and relationships all the days of your life.

Aggressively go after a new life. Don't shrink from it. Don't look back. Identify the people, things, and places that can no longer be part of your new life . . . and *leave the old life behind forever.* Develop a strategy. Be certain that the rate at which you go after this new life will determine how quickly you experience change for good.

At this juncture, you will be ready for something more thorough to keep you focused on the target.

You will be asked to keep a daily, written record of your thoughts, feelings, and progress. When you commit to making time to honestly assess *your* truths, commitments, values, thought life, and more *in writing*, you have black-and-white proof of your pace and direction at every stage of the transformation. At the end of the journey, you will have a book detailing each step of your life.

Daily put your life into perspective. Always, always *hold on to love* to keep you motivated throughout your entire journey.

And no matter what, don't look for an escape. Look for a solution.

Whether you have tried ten times, a hundred times, or a thousand times . . . never, never give up. When you add up the change, you will have a legacy to leave on this earth.

The reason I believe this approach to change is radical is because it will take all you have to give of yourself—physically, emotionally, spiritually, and mentally.

Therefore *Keep the Change* begins, rather than ends, with an unusual and specific request.

I believe that for you to give yourself a true opportunity to launch out of complacency, a rut, or even self-destruction, you need to fully embrace a vision of how you might experience permanent transformation in your life.

I am asking you to make a commitment to read this entire book over a short period of time. In fact, I suggest you consider taking this book to the mountains or to some remote, quiet location for a solitary one-day or weekend retreat. No matter the place, I want you to picture yourself on a trip where you can't go back home to your life as you left it. Therefore, it is time to be honest about your life as it really is . . .

Initially, just by taking the challenge to read the entire book, you will discover how difficult or easy it is for you to finish something you start, especially if at the onset it feels uncomfortable . . . or seems too radical! But as we proceed, you will begin to clearly see your life, your options, and your decisions. You will have a chance to exchange your excuses for new behaviors that will lead to powerful and permanent transformation.

Give me eight chapters of your time . . .
and I will give you compelling illustrations and life-changing examples to inspire and motivate you to hold on to your dreams, achieve your goals, and *keep the change* you deeply desire—today, tomorrow, and permanently.

If you want theory and clinical formulas, you won't find them here. This book took me twenty-five years to write. I am living proof that a dreamer can reach his or her impossible goals and that AN OUT-OF-CONTROL LIFE CAN PERMANENTLY AND POSITIVELY CHANGE.

I will show you a way to keep the change in your life that I know works.

Let's begin . . .

1. E-mail me today (letters@beckytirabassi.com) with your decision: Will you read this entire book? No name or physical address is necessary.

2. Include your start date, and to the best of your ability today, identify, in one sentence, the dream, goal, or struggle in which you long to break through. (If you need help focusing in on the core issue[s], take the self-test that follows.) If a combination of lifestyle changes is involved, please address them all.

3. In the final pages of this book, I will ask you to e-mail me again with your specific plan to keep the desired changes in your life—forever. No correspondence will be published without your permission. No e-mail addresses will be shared with any other company.

Self-Test

To help you identify the areas of your life you need to change, take this short self-test.

1. Is there a habit that is hindering your health or relationships? Examples might be anger, overeating, addiction to alcohol or drugs, or

gambling. Define the problem in a sentence or even in one word.

_____

_____

_____

_____

2. What repeatedly trips you up, stops your progress, or sends you back to the beginning? If you are unwilling or afraid to be honest or are simply blind to yourself, ask someone you trust to explore this with you. If you end up in this place often, it doesn't matter. In order to keep the change you desire, you must start over, again and again, until you overcome.

_____

_____

_____

_____

_____

3. Perhaps you instinctively know that you need a change of heart before you can move forward in your future relationships or in your personal growth. What is the heart change you long to experience? Is it forgiveness toward someone who hurt you or perhaps empathy toward someone who is different

than you? What change of heart do you desire *for a lifetime?* _____

_____

_____

_____

_____

4. Identify your purpose in life as you see it today. _____

_____

_____

_____

_____

5. Now is the time to accept or choose a change of direction in order to move ahead with your life's purpose. Must you acquire more education, relocate, or refocus your efforts before you can truly realize your dreams and potential? What immediate change of direction is necessary for you to fulfill or pursue your potential? _____

_____

_____

_____

_____

6. Is there an attitude that you recognize in yourself as negative, hurtful, stubborn, impatient, arrogant, or destructive in your workplace or home life? To change these attitude patterns, you must be willing to replace an old way of thinking *forever* and respond to others with a more positive, patient way of communicating *forever.* You know that without making this change, you will not have fulfilling, lifelong relationships. What attitude do you resolve to change forever? _____

_____

_____

_____

_____

_____

_____

_____

_____

_____

_____

_____

_____

_____

_____

one

Live to Tell the Truth

While recently waiting in a reception area for a meeting to begin, I began chatting with the only other person waiting for an appointment. Both in New York on business, we discovered that during the same five-year period we had lived about two blocks from each other—back in California!

I asked him what he did for a living and he asked what I did. When I mentioned that I had written a book called *Change Your Life*, I noticed that the young receptionist began to repeatedly look back and glance at me. Finally she caught my eye and said, "I read your book awhile ago."

"You did? Does that mean you are trying to change or improve some area in your life?"

"Kind of . . . ," she said. Then she became quiet.

That didn't exactly answer my question, so I asked her one more: "Are you still trying to change something in your life?"

"Kind of," she acknowledged again.

The Truth about Change

Change is very difficult. It is a process. It is not static. It is ongoing, never ending.

To achieve lasting change is not—and never will be—easy. To think otherwise is naive. To believe otherwise is unrealistic.

If you truly desire to achieve change that lasts, it will require . . .

- ► discomfort for a season,
- ► stretching until you touch new places,
- ► letting go and leaping into the unknown,
- ► pushing out of a comfort zone until living a changed life feels natural,
- ► appearing foolish to other people, but remaining unthreatened by looks of disapproval,
- ► surrendering to a better way,
- ► facing fear until it no longer holds any power . . . however long it takes, and
- ► telling the truth about you to yourself and others.

If you cannot sustain change in your life—if you relapse or fail repeatedly, if you have shelved a dream because of too many rejections—don't give up. BREAKING THROUGH TO PERMANENT TRANSFORMATION CAN BEGIN TODAY IF YOU ARE WILLING TO START WITH THE TRUTH ABOUT YOURSELF AND YOUR SITUATION.

What *is* your truth today?

Does your anger hinder you?

Is your marriage in trouble?

Are your kids spinning out of control?

Are your finances in the tank?

Are you abusing your body?

Is there a dream in your heart that won't go away?

Believing lies, denying the truth, or avoiding reality will keep you from changing your life. Understand that your false beliefs may be holding you back from grasping what you deeply desire.

You must embrace truth. Truth *will* change your life. And not only that, it has intrinsic power to help you keep the change.

YOU CAN RUN, BUT YOU CANNOT HIDE

Many of us run as long as we can before facing the truth. Instead of clearly seeing and admitting the reality of our lives, we buy into the lies.

The lies tell us . . .

- ► we're not really hurting anyone else,
- ► the problem can wait until tomorrow,
- ► people can't really change,
- ► we're merely products of faulty parenting,
- ► we can deal with the issue on our own, or
- ► divorce is the only option.

Just as the details of your life and journey are unique to you, the specific lies you unwittingly believe are not exactly the same as someone else's. The imbalance of lies and truth in your life must be diligently and carefully examined and exposed. This requires identifying the lies you believe, regardless of whether or not those around you see them.

In his counseling practice, my husband, Roger, spends a great deal of time helping clients recognize and throw out the lies that keep them trapped in destructive patterns. He is certain that false beliefs about ourselves, others, or our situations hold us back from lasting, permanent change.

Lies creep in from just about everywhere. Many of the lies you currently believe may come from something your parents taught you. Maybe there is a personal trauma or abuse in your history that caused you to buy a lie. Perhaps your expectations about a given situation caused you to buy a lie. Maybe it's something you heard or a repetitive thought.

Family Ties and Lies

It is not abnormal to grow up in a family where parents are relatively unaware of how their behaviors affect their children. Mothers and fathers are imperfect people who often fall short of meeting the emotional needs of their children.

My husband grew up with parents who truly loved him and did many things to demonstrate their love. But in spite of that, Roger was greatly affected by the anger he saw in his father. The feelings created by his dad's temper caused Roger to fear that his father didn't love him. Despite clear evidence contradicting his belief, once Roger bought into the lie it was nearly impossible to drive it out. The fear brought on by the lie impacted much of his young life.

Roger remembers working in the garage with his dad one day when he was about eleven or twelve years old. Roger's job was to hold a wooden board still while his dad flattened a piece of steel against it with a sledgehammer. As his father raised the hammer to strike the metal, young Roger got scared and took his hands off the board. In his impatience and frustration, Roger's father yelled at him. To this day, Roger remembers thinking, *Now I know my dad doesn't love me.*

Off and on for years, the lie that he was unloved by his father stayed in the back of Roger's mind. While he didn't spend a lot of time consciously thinking about it, he always felt it nagging at him.

Some of the effects that this powerful lie created were hopeless and depressive feelings. It directly affected his self-esteem and the health of many of his relationships. And it certainly hindered his emotional bond with his father, limiting the love he was able to show toward him.

A personal crisis during his twenties led Roger to a counselor's office. Once there, he finally began unpacking all of the lies he had held for so long. At the top of his list of lies was the belief that his father didn't love him. But then came another list: evidence that his father really *did* love him.

Once Roger identified both his faulty beliefs and the truth, he began a journey that led to inner healing, relieved depression, and gave him a better self-image and an improved relationship with his father and others. Exposing the lies ultimately helped

Roger better understand his dad and connect with him on a more loving and transparent level. It gave the two men an opportunity to bridge some of the areas where they felt distant.

TRUTH, LIES, AND CONSEQUENCES

If you are serious about wanting to change for good, you must constantly separate the truth from the lies in your life.

Acknowledging the truth about, rather than buying into or believing, the lies embedded in your mind will require a very radical shift in your perception of your life. TAKING OWNERSHIP OF YOUR LIFE TODAY—WHERE IT IS AND WHERE IT IS GOING—IS YOUR ONLY OPTION. You must identify the faulty beliefs and embrace the truth.

No matter the source of the lies, you will begin to change your life permanently when you identify the lies and discard them for truth. Once you have separated the lies from the truth, you will more clearly understand how your false beliefs have *perpetuated* destructive feelings, botched relationships, unhealthy obsessions, and patterns of failure. This is a powerful and practical method for snapping out of complacency and cycles of negative behaviors.

Do any of these scenarios sound familiar?

You continually scream at your children. Do you really think yelling is the most effective way to discipline them? Has it worked so far? When people scream at *you*, do you feel motivated to change?

You are considering divorce. Do you believe the lie that marriage should be easier and that a vow for life is too hard to keep?

You are stuck in a cycle of starvation and binging. Are you buying into a lie that you are unacceptable unless you look a certain way?

You are unwilling to take a risk that could mean finally achieving your goal. Do you believe the lie that says you're doomed to fail or that your critics might be right?

You are maxed out on five credit cards. Do you believe the lie that says you are already this far into debt and a little more doesn't matter?

You relapsed and lost your sobriety again. Did you buy the lie that said you could handle hanging out with the old crowd?

Change *begins* when you recognize the truth about your life. Permanent change is yours when you let that truth *continually* adjust, improve, and change your behavior.

Though denial, blaming, or making excuses may *initially* be less humiliating than the truth, whenever you resort to these tactics, they will always hinder your progress toward your ultimate goals.

Change that is based on truth, rather than lies, is built on a solid foundation and will last.

Don't delay any longer.

If the truth is that you are stuck, weak, addicted, in trouble, wrong, or need help . . . admit it. Say it out loud. Speak the truth.

Then get on with it by letting the truth change your life.

LIVE LIKE YOU BELIEVE

Consider this novel idea: Let the lies die and begin to *act* like you believe the truth.

If you believed that your screaming was destroying your children's self-esteem, would you still yell?

If you acknowledged that every marriage takes hard work and forgiveness, and that you must still work to rekindle the love, would you still consider divorce?

If you believed the truth that you are more than your outer, physical appearance, would you still punish your body with cruel starvation or overeating?

If you held on to the truth that your dream is your call in life, would you still play it safe and not take the risk?

If you believed that true value isn't found in a new outfit or even a new car, would you still buy them if they put you into debt?

If you believed that, as an addict who wants to be sober, you can't use controlled substances *ever*, would you still tempt fate with a meaningless night on the town?

If you have sunk your teeth into a whole lot of faulty beliefs, it is no surprise that you are not experiencing permanent transformation!

But there is no better day than today . . . or no better time than right now to start living like you believe the truth!

The Truth about . . .

I am going to ask you to look over the following lists of truths and consider their application in your own life. This is your opportunity to step outside yourself and be an observer. If something below exposes a lie in your life, creates discomfort, and even causes embarrassment, mark it and identify how it relates to you, even if looks or sounds ugly. That is exactly what "The Truth about . . . " list is supposed to elicit: an honest, transparent conversation with yourself—about yourself. Some of the areas may seem more relevant to you than others, but go ahead and read through each of them and think through them as you go.

At the end of each section, take a moment to respond to the questions as you identify the lies and replace them with truth in your life.

THE TRUTH ABOUT ANGER

Unhealthy expressions and emotions such as anger can be as harmful and crippling as any physical addiction. Acknowledging the truth about the impact of anger on yourself and those around you might be extremely powerful in helping you begin to heal and change.

Mark any of the following truths that relate to you:

_____ Anger that is out of control will hurt, demean, separate, and even destroy relationships.

_____ Anger can result in physical and emotional illness.

_____ My anger isolates me.

_____ Anger can be controlled, and emotional abuse can be healed over time and with great humility.

_____ I have a problem with controlling my temper, language, or level and my tone of voice with _____. This is an unacceptable way of communication.

_____ I am in close relationships with some angry people and have learned some hurtful ways of communicating my thoughts and feelings with people I know—and even with those I don't know.

_____ I am wholly responsible for my emotions.

_____ I will not be successful in changing this area of my life without outside help and accountability. I must get professional help and/or join a support group until those around me whom I have hurt with my anger agree that I have made significant progress.

The lie I am exposing about my anger is _____

_____

_____

_____

_____

The real truth about my anger is _____

_____

_____

_____

_____

This truth must affect the following behavior: _____

_____

_____

_____

_____

THE TRUTH ABOUT ALCOHOL, DRUGS, AND SEX

Addicts must accept the truth about the power of addiction. This belief will turn into a behavior when they make a non-negotiable decision to quit, abstain, or stop "using" today and forever. If they insist on holding on to the lie that tells them they can be moderate or return to "using" after a specified period of time, they will not experience sobriety for a lifetime. Sobriety requires a complete and total change in your perception of the truth. Complete abstinence is the only way for addicts to experience their goal of permanent transformation. Instead of making a vague attempt to "cut back," addicts must make a specific decision—based on the truth—to abstain forever. Otherwise, permanent transformation remains elusive, and setbacks and relapses are guaranteed.

Keep the Change

If you struggle with an addiction to drugs, alcohol, or sex, this may be the first or the fiftieth time you are acknowledging your struggle. Today, see how many of the following statements ring true in your life. Fill in the blanks to identify your particular struggle(s). No matter your past mistakes, if you desire to move forward, you must be truthful about your present.

I am addicted to ＿＿＿＿＿＿＿＿＿.

Staying away from ＿＿＿＿＿＿＿＿ is a problem for me. I have not been willing or able to abstain from this up until this point, yet I desire to do so.

I can't seem to let go of it. It has a hold on me. Therefore, I want to change my behavior in regard to ＿＿＿＿＿＿＿＿.

This has hurt my relationships and affected many areas of my life such as ＿＿＿＿＿＿＿＿＿＿＿＿.

If I control or abstain from ＿＿＿＿＿＿＿＿, a number of important relationships will immediately improve in my life (spouse, friends, coworkers, children, etc.).

If I abstain from ＿＿＿＿＿＿＿＿, I will relieve myself of the constant pressure of maintaining moderation . . . a line I cross over occasionally/regularly/often.

If I abstain from ＿＿＿＿＿＿＿＿, I will have to change some/many/most of my friends with whom I spend time and some/many/most of the places I go.

If I abstain from ＿＿＿＿＿＿＿＿, I will stop the generational abuse/addiction and set an example of sobriety for all my family members.

12

If I abstain from_____, I will gain respect for myself from others.

If I abstain from_____, I must tell others of my decision (instead of hiding or avoiding it.)

In order to abstain from_____, I must attend support meetings for those who struggle with abuse and keep an honest account of my consecutive days of sobriety. I must become accountable to one person who will be my sponsor.

If I abstain from_____, I will have new freedoms that I deeply desire. I will be able to build and rebuild important relationships, spend my time differently, and (personalize for your unique situation) _____

_____

_____

_____

The lie I am exposing about my addiction is _____

_____

_____

_____

The real truth about this area is _____

_____

_____

_____

This truth must affect the following behavior: _____

_____

_____

THE TRUTH ABOUT MY BODY

Unless an overweight person accepts the truth that he or she must watch how often and how much he or she eats and is willing to exercise regularly, lasting change in body shape and size will remain forever elusive.

Mark any of the following truths that relate to you:

_____ Everyone has a certain body type, metabolism, height, and shape that is unique to him or her and is influenced by his or her genetics.

_____ Food is intended to fuel the body, and exercise releases energy and burns calories as a part of its function. People who fuel their body according to its needs (and not in excess) will maintain a healthier weight for their height.

_____ I have unhealthy obsessions about food and exercise such as _____

_____

_____

I struggle to control my weight because _____

_____

_____

_____ I have struggled to find the right amount of exercise and the appropriate amount of food intake since (age/date)

_____

_____ Short-term, yo-yo diets and fad fitness plans do not work for me. In order to decrease inches or weight, I must reduce my caloric intake and increase my calorie-burning activities.

_____ Weight management cannot be considered a short-term goal.

_____ I must get outside help to develop a healthy eating and exercise plan that is realistic and specific to my life, age, income, and goals.

_____ I must attend regular support meetings and/or exercise classes where someone keeps me accountable to my goals.

_____ Paying attention to my daily eating and exercise habits is a healthy, manageable, and very successful way to achieve and maintain permanent weight loss.

_____ I can no longer make excuses for myself.

The lie I am exposing about my body is _____

_____

_____

_____

The real truth about my body is _____

_____

_____

_____

This truth must affect the following behavior: _____

_____

_____

_____

_____

THE TRUTH ABOUT PROCRASTINATION

If procrastinators understand the consequences of their behavior but refuse to admit the truth about their dismal time-management habits and the negative effect on themselves and others, they will continually, perpetually, repeatedly fall back into their old patterns. If they are unwilling to live by the truth and change their time-management habits immediately, they will not see permanent transformation in their life today or tomorrow. Change begins with incorporating the truth through behavior modification today and continues through tomorrow, the next day, and the next.

Mark any of the following truths that relate to you:

_____ Delaying, postponing, and putting off projects and/or being continuously late for meetings, classes, work, and appointments are self-destructive and selfish behaviors.

_____ Habitual procrastination and/or tardiness will result in difficulties in my workplace and relationships.

_____ I am not realistic about the time it takes for me to complete a project, from start to finish, or about the amount of time it takes to get somewhere.

_____ I have to change my behavior and my attitude about respecting and honoring other people's time as much as I do my own.

_____ I must get up earlier. This might require setting more than one alarm clock and/or hiring a wake-up phone service.

_____ I must start a project earlier in the day or week than I have done previously. I must set my due date earlier than the final due date in order to give myself a little more room to complete the project.

_____ I cannot allow interruptions to steal my focus. Therefore I have to turn off the television until I finish my work.

_____ I have to turn off the telephone and/or let the answering machine take calls and then return them only after I have met my project goals for the hour or the day.

_____ I will set rules about reading or responding to e-mail or web searching until a project is completed for the day.

_____ I will notify my friends that I'm temporarily unavailable, asking them not to spontaneously invite me to join them in activities we enjoy until my deadline is met.

Procrastination and tardiness can be lifelong problems. In order to achieve permanent transformation in this area of my life, I will have to work at it and fight for it daily. But the personal and professional results of a changed life will mean improved relationships and productivity.

The lie I am exposing about procrastination is _____

_____

_____

_____

The real truth about my procrastination is _____

_____

_____

This truth must affect the following behavior: _____

_____

_____

_____

_____

THE TRUTH ABOUT PARENTING

If parents continually scream and yell at their children, exhibiting out-of-control, demeaning behavior, the children will gradually lose respect for authority. Parents who fail to act on the truth about the damage they are causing will continue to speak rudely and negatively toward their children. The consequences of failing to remember this truth will not only teach their children poor communication skills but also severely impair the children's self-esteem. The parents also risk losing an affectionate and loving adult relationship with their children. The lie wins.

Mark any of the following truths that relate to you:

_____ Parenting is a lifelong adventure.

_____ As a parent, I am a caretaker of my child. How I speak, touch, encourage, discipline, and mentor him or her should come from a place of love and patience.

_____ Every child is an individual who will learn and grow at different stages because of his or her unique personality and genetic makeup.

_____ What works for one child will not necessarily work for another child.

_____ I must seek to understand my child's strengths and personality and build him or her up with encouragement.

_____ My child should be treated with the same kindness, control, and respect with which I desire to be treated.

_____ I alone am responsible for my emotions.

The lie I am exposing about my role as a parent is _____

_____

_____

The truth about parenting that I must embrace is _____

_____

_____

This truth must affect the following behavior: _____

_____

_____

_____

THE TRUTH ABOUT MARRIAGE

If spouses fail to acknowledge the truth about their individual roles in the marriage and are continually critical, unwilling to invest time in the marriage relationship, workaholics, and perpetually stubborn, self-centered, dishonest, or unfaithful, there is little chance they will enjoy marriage for a lifetime.

Mark any of the following truths that relate to you.

_____ Marriage is a union of two individuals who make a decision to live together and love each other for a lifetime.

_____ My spouse will never fulfill all of my needs, nor is he or she perfect.

_____ I will never fulfill all of my spouse's needs, nor am I perfect.

_____ Marriage requires 100 percent effort and flexibility on my part.

_____ Marriage is a union of two forgivers. The act of forgiveness in marriage means we cannot let the sun go down on our anger.

_____ My refusal to forgive is at the root of much of our problem.

_____ A marriage vow is a decision to never have an intimate relationship with anyone other than my spouse. This means that even entertaining the idea of infidelity is a serious breach of my marriage covenant.

_____ The marriage vows are not only for the wedding day. Loving and cherishing my spouse, in sickness and in health, for richer or poorer, until death parts us, is a nonnegotiable part of my commitment.

_____ Divorce is not an act of convenience. To think otherwise is terribly selfish and destructive toward my spouse, our children, and those whom we love as friends and family.

The lie I am exposing about my views on marriage is _____

_____

_____

_____

The real truth I commit to believing today about marriage is

_____

_____

_____

This truth must affect the following behavior: _____

_____

_____

_____

_____

THE TRUTH ABOUT FORGIVENESS

Forgiveness is designed to heal, absolve, and restore our physical and emotional health. As you extend forgiveness, a sense of release and freedom will occur within your own soul. Honesty with yourself about your own imperfections may give you room to extend grace to those who hurt you.

Mark any of the following truths that relate to you:

_____ Unforgiveness has the power to destroy my health.

_____ Forgiveness is a powerful tool for reconciliation. It is rarely earned or deserved. It is a gift that is given.

_____ Forgiveness is not a feeling but a decision.

_____ Forgiveness extended toward someone who has hurt me will free me.

_____ To withhold forgiveness is to give my offender control over me.

_____ I know that the greater debt I forgive, the greater love I will release.

_____ Forgiving others is difficult.

_____ I hold grudges. I would rather seek revenge before offering forgiveness. I want to wound or hurt the person who hurts me. But I know instinctively that forgiveness will release us both from this place of distance and discord.

_____ My inability to forgive _____ is taking a toll on my physical and emotional health.

_____ Receiving forgiveness can change a life forever. I want to experience permanent transformation in my life, therefore I will commit to a lifestyle of short accounts and daily forgiveness.

The lie I am exposing about my inability to forgive is _____

_____

_____

_____

The real truth I must embrace and hold on to about forgiveness is _____

_____

_____

This truth must affect the following behavior: _____

_____

_____

_____

_____

THE TRUTH ABOUT FAILURE

A common thread of those who desire to overcome, achieve, or dream is a fear of failure. The most wonderful gift you can give yourself is the truth about failure! See it as permission to keep going.

Mark any of the following truths that relate to you.

_____ Failure is not a person but an experience.

_____ The power I give to my failure determines how I face risk, opportunity, relationships, and the unknown.

_____ Successful people encounter failure in small and large ways. How quickly I get back on my feet after failing determines how quickly or slowly—if at all—I will move forward again.

_____ Though a stumble is costly and humbling, what I learn from my own mistakes and failures often provides the next _enlightened_ step in my progress.

_____ Learning from others' mistakes and failures saves time, money, and heartache.

_____ Putting myself in an atmosphere, as well as providing one, where lessons are learned—without loss of relationship—will move us all in positive direction.

_____ I must treat someone who fails with the same graciousness and compassionate treatment I would like to receive if the roles were reversed.

My thoughts about failure affect my life and the lives of those around me. They are: _____

_____

_____

_____

_____ If I overcome my fears, I can encourage others to overcome the fear of failure by _____

_____

_____

_____

_____ Failure is a part of the journey of life.
The lie I am exposing about failure is _____

_____

_____

_____

The truth I must embrace about failure is _____

_____

_____

_____

_____

This truth must affect the following behavior: _____

_____

_____

_____

_____

_____

THE TRUTH ABOUT FAITH

Faith believes what you cannot see.

Faith is being sure of what you hope for.

Faith appears foolish to some.

Faith is the antidote for fear.

Without faith, it is impossible to please God.

The lie I have believed about faith is _____

_____

_____

_____

The truth I must embrace about faith is _____

_____

_____

_____

This truth must affect the following behavior: _____

_____

_____

DON'T BUY THE LIES

Why do some people make progress and then slip backward so quickly? Most likely, they have not faced the lies about their lives and then implemented the truth into their character, situation, and circumstances. Changing your behavior on the outside won't miraculously wipe out the lies you believe. But replacing the lies with truth *will* change your behavior.

If you are unable to achieve or sustain change in your life at a counselor's suggestion, through your own good intentions, or even after receiving an ultimatum, perhaps your roadblock is that you have not yet believed the truth with the same ferocity as you have believed the lies.

I am absolutely convinced that if you will . . .
accept and embrace the truth about yourself and your personal struggles, and acknowledge exactly how your behavior must change, your personal struggle will lose power over you—*beginning right now*. If you *continue* to face the truth, you will continue to change.

What truths must you admit in order for this area of your life to change? _____

_____

_____

_____

What behaviors must change if you are to fully embrace the truth and reject the lies? _____

_____

_____

_____

What are your greatest fears about changing your behavior?

_____

_____

_____

_____

How does the truth affect those fears? _____

_____

_____

_____

Live to Tell the Truth!

If you have still not identified the area (or areas) of your life that express the truth about you, then use the space below to define the truth as you know it. Be honest and transparent. Reread what you have written and rephrase any lies or excuses. If you are ashamed of yourself and worried about someone else reading what you write, feel free to use abbreviations or other ways of writing that only you can understand. But before moving on, I ask you to sincerely expose the lies in your life and separate them from the truth. Then list any behaviors that must change for you to achieve permanent, lasting change in this area (or areas) of your life. Use extra journal paper if you need more space.

The truth about me: _____

_____

_____

_____

_____

_____

_____

_____

_____

_____

_____

_____

_____

_____

_____

_____

_____

_____

_____

_____

_____

_____

_____

_____

_____

_____

_____

_____

_____

Only if you embrace the truth will you live to tell it.

two

Harness Your Pain

I wish I could sidestep this chapter, but I can't. Pain is a part of everyone's life and journey—and it has a very important purpose. If harnessed it can become an *essential* motivator in lasting change. If ignored, it won't be silent and will likely create more pain. But if we will listen and learn, pain will teach us something very important.

In C. S. Lewis's book *The Problem of Pain*, he says, "God whispers to us in our pleasures, speaks in our conscience, but shouts in our pain." If you are hearing the shouting, or even trying to drown it out, you very well may be hindering your own progress toward permanent transformation.

Hitting Bottom, Looking Up

The term *hitting bottom* is a word picture that describes the jarring, painful crash of one who has fallen into a deep hole and landed hard.

The fall feels even worse when we ourselves dig the very holes into which we plummet!

It is not uncommon to slip and slide down a dark tunnel

for weeks, months, or even years before the fall is broken. Reaching the bottom is often preceded by countless occasions of repeated poor behavior that results in the destruction of relationships or careers. Time after time we take risks and chances—not thinking, not caring, and never expecting the worst will really happen—until it finally does.

In this place, we are alone, angry, afraid, and overwhelmed. Disgust, shame, and real pain are the end results.

For many of us, it is only then, at the bottom, that we cry, "No more!" When we finally acknowledge that we can't go any lower, there is only one thing we can do. Instead of letting the pain push us backward, this is the moment we must instinctively grab on to an invisible hand.

In my own life, I can give you details of just about every one of my "bottomed-out" moments. In fact, in most cases, I can give you the exact day. They were that memorable—and extremely painful.

To this day I vividly remember the emotional pain and shame I experienced during a five-year period of binge drinking, drug addiction, and promiscuous sex. On many occasions, I woke up not remembering where I had left my car the night before. More than once I crashed a car while drinking, but even that was not enough to keep me from drinking and driving. I repeatedly took risks and chances with drugs and alcohol, not thinking, not caring, and never expecting the worst to happen . . . until it did.

One morning I woke up in an unfamiliar place lying next to a guy I barely knew. I had lost track of my friends, and I had no recollection of what I had done with this man the night before.

That morning, I was nauseated, angry, afraid of the consequences, and overwhelmed. But the intense mixture of regret and shame acted like a spotlight on a very dark room in and out of which I'd spent many years wandering. The intense feelings triggered by this experience finally exposed what was in the room: out-of-control binge drinking, illegal drugs, and immorality. I was disgusted in what and who I had become—an addict.

In that moment, a dramatic shift occurred. THE SHEER VOLUME OF EMOTIONAL PAIN THAT OVERWHELMED ME WAS SUDDENLY STRONGER THAN MY NEED TO ABUSE ALCOHOL OR USE DRUGS. In fact, I remember thinking, *I will commit suicide and end my life before I let alcohol and drugs control me any longer.*

If, up to that point, I was naive, in denial, in a stupor, or oblivious to the consequences of my drinking, I finally woke up that day. I point to that experience as the most humiliating moment of my entire life. The pain of being so deeply ashamed, with no one to blame but myself, finally gave me the reason and resolve to change my life.

That was a defining day. To acknowledge that I was an alcoholic was extremely painful. But instead of letting the searing pain push me backward, it actually provided me with the strength to overcome the addictions. I finally stopped the pattern of abuse. I knew I was not meant to be an alcoholic, immoral, and foulmouthed. But I had to turn from it—or die from it. I instinctively knew that if I didn't change then, the incredible emotional pain and personal humiliation would take me deeper.

The shame turned into determination that got me through the first hour of abstinence. Then it kept me sober throughout the first day and eventually carried me through an entire week. Remembering that pain sustained my commitment to change even during the hardest times.

Over twenty-five years later, those addictions have no control over my life because I refuse to forget the overwhelming, shameful, and spun-out feelings of being out of control. The power of temptation is more easily defeated each time I choose to remember those feelings of pain and despair and let them keep me tightly tethered to my path of change.

The hardest fall in my life was on the day I admitted that I was an alcoholic. That day of self-disclosure was very painful and humiliating. Yet I have something to show for it. The shock and trauma of hitting bottom led to an unwavering commitment to sobriety.

There were several other explosions in my life that did not leave me dead but changed me for the better.

SPUN OUT

On a spring day in 1983, I completely "spun out" as a screaming, hollering mother. I yelled at my son so loudly that I am pretty sure the neighbors heard me. Immediately afterward I was ashamed and embarrassed. I sat down to journal, and I recorded a very poignant thought that entered my mind. It was simple: "Keep it up and your son will grow up to hate you." I even remember where I was sitting. I was so afraid of ruining my relationship with my son forever that I wrote, "I will never, ever do this again."

Later that night, in front of my husband and son, I confessed that I was prone to out-of-control anger. I asked them to hold me accountable. And believe me, they both kept me accountable! Over twenty years later, I have a fun, nurturing relationship with my son, who, most importantly, has forgiven me.

BALANCING ACT

By the time I was twenty-nine years old, I was losing the struggle with time management, finances, completing projects, and the battle of the bulge. The physical, emotional, spiritual, and mental areas of my life were clearly out of control and affecting several relationships. Then I attended a seminar, not on how to change, but on how to pray. It was rather unusual for me to choose to attend something so serious, but I was desperate to change.

On a Saturday in February 1984, in a hotel convention center in Chicago, I decided I would rather change for good than keep failing at the balancing act. I was miserable and ashamed of myself. I decided, then and there, to stop the pain. My only plan to get a handle on all the areas of my life was this: to journal one-hour daily for the rest of my life. Over nineteen years later, I still spend one hour every day journaling and talking to God about how to fulfill my dreams, heal my relationships, and achieve a healthy body. And without reservation, I would suggest that THIS ONE DISCIPLINE, FORGED OUT OF PAIN, HAS CHANGED MY LIFE MORE THAN ANY OTHER HABIT IN MY LIFE.

APPETITE TIGHTROPE

I also remember when I finally hit bottom with food. At the time, it was an all-consuming obsession in my life. I could not stop thinking about it or binging. It controlled my schedule, social activities, and flexibility. I was jealous of those who were thin. And my jealousy turned into comparison, irritability, anger, and more binging. One day I woke up and said, "I've had enough."

With the help of some friends and family, I gave up the fads and diets and began following a daily plan that included regular exercise and healthy eating. I didn't lose the weight quickly, but

I kept off what I lost. Neither my metabolism nor my appetite changed overnight, but when I decided that I would no longer merely *think* about the issue, I began to *do* something about it daily. I began to daily record two action steps: what I planned to eat and when I would exercise during the week.

The emotional obsession and unhappiness that comes with being overweight is something I never want to experience again.

If you are at the bottom, do not give in to hopelessness or despair. The bottom is the place where great power is waiting for release in your life. If you are at this place and you have no other choice, then claim this as a defining moment. Harness the pain and *make the decision* to change for good.

If you struggle with pride, you will probably be a bottom hitter. But there is only one way up and out of a pit. At the bottom, you must humbly admit you have a problem, then grab a hand and ask for help.

Working through the Pain

Last night I had dinner with my friend Karen. In 1995, at the age of twenty-five, she almost drowned in her bathtub after passing out from too much drinking. She awoke with lungs full of water and black eyes. When she looked in the mirror, she finally came face to face with the truth about herself. I was one of the first people she called, and we traveled cross-country to meet. I was one hand she grabbed to lift her up and off the bottom.

Sober eight years now, she is well down the road of recovery.

She contends that her changed life is a slow work in progress. She admits that she had to aggressively pursue it, that it didn't chase her.

To those who don't know her, she has a beautiful family and appears to have "everything." But she is really a woman who experienced great pain and lived to tell the truth! And she has never forgotten the humiliation and deceit of her life as an out-of-control alcoholic.

She is refreshingly honest and transparent. Because she has steadily worked through the pain, she radiates humility.

Now a wife and mother, Karen is still supported by a woman who became her accountability partner eight years ago. Though their phone calls have decreased from daily to once a month, the two women remain connected. Karen is also a support person in a younger woman's life. Both relationships keep her aware of her vulnerability, as well as her progress. She still regularly attends two to three support meetings each week and regularly attends church on Sundays. In addition, she says that she "checks in regularly with God throughout the day."

I asked Karen, "Do you ever think about the day you hit bottom?"

Without hesitation she said, "I keep my 'bottom' very close to me." She said, "In fact, working through the pain of my alcoholism is what caused the greatest paradigm shift in my life. It didn't happen overnight, but what has changed the most in me are my desires—what I want and what I worship."

What a powerful way to look at pain!

Pain brings clarity to your life, perhaps like nothing else. In fact, pain has a lasting effect on our lives that joy and celebration simply do not achieve. It can deeply, significantly change both our aspirations and our character.

That defining day when Karen looked in the mirror, she realized she was not a woman of integrity or faith or character. It was a painful realization, but it caused her to finally give up alcohol and go after what mattered in life.

Unique Pain

Some strugglers won't have to experience a total meltdown (by others' standards) before they are propelled to change their life. Many people have such a low emotional pain tolerance that the minute they are out of alignment they quickly look for ways to make adjustments. Even how people respond to pain, or the amount of pain it takes to catch their attention, has a lot to do with personality types, as we'll see in the next chapter.

Take, for instance, substance abuse. Some people have no limiting mechanism and exhibit a greater tolerance. Others who encounter a substance for the first time may wake up the next morning with a hangover and swear off it for the rest of their life.

Some may be extremely shy. For them, there is no greater pain than public humiliation. The discomfort will affect them tremendously and cause them to isolate themselves or with-draw from others for weeks. Others might shake it off or even laugh over the very same incident.

And while some people buckle in shame at correction, others are more stubborn and can tolerate much more pain. Every-one around them can shout out warnings, begging them to slow down, turn around, or face reality. But until they hit a wall, they are less likely to voluntarily acknowledge that there is a need to change their behavior.

When it comes to pain, you cannot compare stories with the people next to you and judge the depth of their pain against yours. You know what hurts you. You know how much you can endure before you wave your white flag. Don't diminish the reality of your experience of pain because it doesn't live up to the horror stories of people hanging off the ledge. Pain is pain; you may not always control how and why you experience it, but you certainly have a say in what you do with that pain.

Ineffective Pain Blockers

One of the greatest hindrances to personal growth is trying to cover up pain when it enters your life. My husband tells his clients, "The result of ignoring pain is more pain." In other words, the longer you pretend the pain isn't there, the longer you must wait for healing and restoration to take place. In the meantime, you sentence yourself to endure your current torment. Pain is often there for a reason. It has something to tell you, and until you let it in and hear what it has to say, it will keep scratching at your back door.

There are at least two main ways people respond to their pain. The first is through blaming. Diffusing the responsibility onto others is a quick, easy way to dodge the bullet. Who do you blame when things aren't going well? Your dysfunctional parents? Your demanding boss? Your selfish spouse? Your misbehaving children? An unfair God?

I am not diminishing the fact that other people's behavior can definitely hurt and affect us. But stop yourself the next time you are tempted to blame others for your pain with phrases like, "If it weren't for you, I wouldn't be in this situation." Blaming may make you feel better initially, but it eventually leads to feeling helpless. The truth is, turning the responsibility for your life over to other people's actions will keep you stuck in the role of a victim. As long as you maintain that attitude, you won't take the necessary steps to change.

Roger says that many people get caught up in the cycle of blaming others. They ask, "Why did they do this to me?" The sooner they can ask themselves the better question—"What's next? How can I keep moving?"—they are able to move out of the pain and on toward healing.

Numbing is another way people respond to pain. IF YOU CHOOSE TO NUMB THE PAIN, YOU ARE SIMPLY DELAYING THE HEALING. Remember, ignoring your pain will only result in more pain.

Think about a woman who gets lost in romance novels. On the surface, this seems like an innocuous example. But consider this: Do you think this ultimately helps her feel less lonely? Does her fantasy in any way fill the void of her loneliness? Yes, but only temporarily. In the end she is still left longing for the real thing.

If she would acknowledge her pain and express her honest feelings about loneliness, then she could begin to move out of the pain. By uncovering what is beneath the pain, she can move away from the novels and fill her need for companionship with real relationships. Instead of isolating herself, she needs to find intimate relationships. She might find time to join a bicycling club, volunteer with a community or church organization, or meet up with friends at a party. These activities provide a lot more hope and potential for curing her lonely heart.

Finding Purpose in Pain

Pain has shaped and ignited some of the noblest causes. Stories of courage give us hope and inspiration to find purpose from our own pain.

Candy Lightner's personal tragedy led to a change in the way an entire nation looked at drinking and driving. After her daughter was killed by a drunk driver, Candy formed Mothers Against Drunk Driving (MADD). Since then, the organization has successfully fought to make our roads safer by raising awareness and lobbying for tougher drunk-driving laws. Hundreds of lives have undoubtedly been saved.

As a former First Lady, Betty Ford's brave admission that she was an addict shocked the nation. She is credited with bringing the issues of addiction and recovery out into the open. Today, the Betty Ford Center is one of the leading substance-abuse treatment facilities in the country.

In 1981, John Walsh's six-year-old son, Adam, was kidnapped and brutally murdered. He and his wife poured their grief into both driving new legislation through Congress and in founding the Adam Walsh Child Resource Center. Walsh's powerful role as an advocate for missing children led to his well-known position as the host of the *America's Most Wanted* television series. Walsh's work on the show is credited with the apprehension of countless criminals and child abductors.

Charles Colson is best known for his role in the Watergate scandal while serving as an aid to President Nixon. Prior to beginning a prison sentence for his involvement in the scandal, Colson became a Christian. His experiences while incarcerated caused him to emerge as an influential advocate of reforming the criminal justice system. In 1976, he founded Prison Fellowship Ministries—the world's largest outreach to prisoners, crime victims, and the families involved.

Nancy Brinker's sister, Susan Goodman Komen, lost her battle with breast cancer at the age of thirty-six. Keeping a promise she made before her sister died, Nancy established the Susan G. Komen Breast Cancer Foundation in 1982 with just a few hundred dollars in her pocket. After defeating her own battle with breast cancer, Nancy remains committed to funding new research to eradicate the disease. To date, the Komen Foundation has raised more than $300 million.

In 1967, a diving accident left young Joni Eareckson Tada a quadriplegic. Today Joni is a best-selling author and a sought-after speaker, respected painter, and disability advocate. Her organization, Joni and Friends, meets the needs of thousands of disabled people every year.

Lisa Beamer was launched into the nation's spotlight after her husband, Todd, died as a hero on United Flight 93 on September 11, 2001. Just days after the tragedy, she founded the Todd M. Beamer Foundation to help children cope with family trauma. She is the author of a best-selling book about her husband's faith and courage and now travels the country speaking about her hope in the midst of loss.

Helen Keller was left deaf and blind from an illness at the age of two. Overcoming incredible odds to learn how to communicate, Helen went on to astonish the world with her brilliant mind and passionate work on behalf of disabled people.

In the prime of his life, well-loved actor Michael J. Fox was diagnosed with Parkinson's disease. Today he is a powerful advocate for finding a cure for the disease he battles. He taped his final episode of the television series *Spin City* in 2001, and during the same year, he started the Michael J. Fox Foundation for Parkinson's Research.

Remember the Pain

If you hit bottom or got roughed up during a tough period in your life, odds are the experience left a few battle scars.

I am not suggesting that you allow this habit of remembering your pain to turn into an opportunity to wallow in self-pity or that you should continually berate yourself for your mistakes. Neither will self-condemnation or unforgiveness move you toward lasting change. Instead, I urge you to use your very memorable, powerful, and painful feelings to move you toward the life you want to live.

Remember, every person experiences humiliation, shame, or setbacks.

If today you realize you are not who you were meant to be or who you want to be . . . this can be a very painful place of self-discovery.

But I believe THE PAIN AND HUMILIATION OF A HARD FALL, OF TRAGIC CIRCUMSTANCES, OR OF AN UNBELIEVABLY IRRESPONSIBLE MISTAKE IS, IN FACT, YOUR TICKET *OUT* OF THE MESS. I encourage you to grab on to these tickets; let them be your *reasons* to quit, stop, wake up, rebound, reverse your direction, and never return to an unhealthy lifestyle.

Over time, as you allow pain to give you courage, shape you, inspire you, turn you toward faith, and develop humility, you—and others—will see pain remarkably and permanently transform your life and make a difference in your world.

The most poignant and painful moments in your life are seared into your memory. Once you stop trying to suppress the pain, you have an amazing opportunity to use it for good in a way that elicits faith, courage, and humility. Allow those memories to ignite enough fire in your muscles to move your body and prompt you to take new, right, and positive action steps. Permit them to spin the wheels of your mind to make better, constructive choices on a daily basis.

What is the greatest pain in your life right now? _____

_____

_____

_____

_____

_____

_____

What are ways you could use your experience of pain to pursue a passion or purpose in your life? _____

_____

_____

_____

_____

_____

What is a specific moment in your life when intense feelings of regret, shame, embarrassment, or pain revealed your need to change something about yourself? _____

_____

_____

_____

_____

Describe in detail the way this event or experience made you feel about yourself. _____

_____

_____

_____

_____

_____

What promise to yourself did you make as a result of your feelings? _____

_____

_____

_____

_____

How does remembering those feelings make you feel about the truth of your situation today? _____

_____

_____

_____

_____

List ways that you block your pain. _____

_____

_____

_____

_____

_____

Are you blaming anyone for the pain you feel? If so, who?

_____

_____

_____

_____

_____

Instead of blaming, write down what steps you will take to move on. _____

_____

_____

_____

_____

_____

What is the pain in your life you are trying to numb? _____

_____

_____

_____

_____

_____

What are some of the ways you attempt to numb that pain?

_____

_____

_____

_____

_____

_____

Mark the ways you might respond instead of numbing the pain.

_____ Join a support group

_____ Call a friend for support

_____ See a counselor, pastor, or psychologist

_____ Read a book on this area in which I'm hurting

_____ Journal about my feelings

_____ Other (explain) _____

_____

_____

_____

_____

_____

_____

_____

_____

_____

_____

Tame Your Temperament

How you . . .

- ► exercise
- ► deal with anger
- ► study
- ► communicate
- ► shop
- ► eat
- ► parent
- ► organize
- ► overcome obstacles . . .

has *everything* to do with how you will keep the change in your life.

Damage Control

Tim LaHaye, author of *The Power of Temperament*, wrote, "Humanly speaking, nothing has a more profound influence on your behavior than your inherited temperament. The combination of your parents' genes and chromosomes at conception, which determined your basic temperament nine months before you drew your first breath, is largely responsible for your actions, reactions, emotional responses, and, to one degree or another, almost everything you do."

It doesn't take long before we realize that we are imperfect —and much of what makes us who we are is out of our control; but who we become with the personality and traits we are given is a matter of learning to control our personality. Doing so can make a tremendous difference as you improve, change, or balance your life. Acknowledging your weak spots, enhancing your strengths, and understanding how you relate to the world around you can help you turn a crucial corner in achieving lasting breakthrough.

Wrecking Ball

In the summer of 2000, we sold our house and bought an older home that needed a complete remodel. We had only six weeks to finish the job and make the move.

I remember how the plans, meetings, and budgetary considerations soon consumed our every waking hour. When my coworkers at the office began calling my cell and home phones to find me, I finally turned the phones off in order to focus on the remodel. When they could not reach me by phone, they faxed me with urgent requests for answers to a variety of concerns.

As I recall—and of course, this was my self-centered perception of the day—I finally stormed into the office and unloaded all of my frustration on my staff. "Stop calling me! Quit looking for me! I'll call you. I'll check in when I can. This remodel is overwhelming, and it's my first priority," I stated with steely eyes and a firm voice.

One coworker seated with me at the conference table responded differently. After thirty minutes of tangling over an issue, I had leveled our meeting to tears. My director of marketing at the time began to cry. I had hurt her. She was a diligent and conscientious worker. She knew I requested approval of most expenditures and event coordination. She was only doing her job.

When I finally realized what I had done—unloaded my personal frustrations on my office coworkers—I was humiliated. I lowered my chin and released hot, irrepressible tears.

It was too late to retreat or reenter the office and start over. I had been impulsive, inconsiderate, and self-centered. I, the leader of the "change your life" message, had miserably failed to exhibit even a small measure of maturity or self-control in my own company, much less the world I am compelled to change for the better.

I INSTINCTIVELY KNEW THE NEXT STEP. I HAD TO APOLOGIZE. Instead, I wanted to walk out. And I would have, but something wouldn't let me. I wish I could say it was humility, but I actually think it was pride.

I looked up, took a breath, and then asked her to forgive me. I said, "I am sorry. I didn't walk in this door intending to make you cry. Will you forgive me?"

Without reservation she said, "Yes."

More than an apology was expected of me. Change was required. I had to stop behaving in such an unprofessional and immature manner.

Even though it was a crushing blow to my ego, I was forced to acknowledge what others knew about me all along: I was very self-centered and full of anger. That was the truth, and it was a painful realization. I felt as if my credibility was damaged. I felt ashamed.

The problem was, I didn't bother remembering the misery of that moment beyond a mere twenty-four hours.

The next day, escrow closed on our new house. With only six weeks to complete our remodel, we requested that the demolition begin with a full crew *at noon* on the day we took official ownership of the property.

At 2:00 P.M., the contractor showed up—alone. The piercing look I gave him was fueled by pure anger and impatience. I couldn't have been more upset. Mindful of the events of the previous day, I held my tongue. But inside I was furious.

Fortunately, my husband appeared at the doorway just as I was receiving the news from the contractor that the project was not starting that day. I decided I should let my husband handle the situation. I made a frustrated sound and stormed out the front door.

My husband immediately followed me down the walkway and into the street. He said, "You just can't leave like that. You can't just walk away from someone in the middle of a conversation. That type of outburst is unacceptable."

"Oh, yeah?" I said. "You think *that* was an outburst?! You should have seen me yesterday! *That* was an outburst! I am using incredible self-control by leaving this situation. Besides, I am doing the only thing I can do to refrain from hitting that guy! I am frustrated and angry and disappointed." I got into my car, slammed my foot on the gas, and left in a puff of smoke.

DEMOLITION CREW

Despite the severity of my anger in both situations, I almost ignored the entire issue one more time. That weekend, Carissa, a former employee, was visiting from northern California and spent the night at our house.

Sitting around the breakfast table the following morning, we replayed the week's activities . . . including my colorful, even humorous, version of the office debacle and the contractor blowup. It is amazing how quickly I brushed aside the very real pain I both felt and caused in each of these instances. Already, I was joking about it and expecting everyone else to join in the laughter.

Most innocently, Carissa looked at my husband and asked, "What would a person like Becky have to do to stop losing control of her emotions?"

What I read into her question was, *For as long as I have known Becky, she has had an anger problem. Can she ever change? Will she always be a fuse ready to light up and explode at any given moment?*

I was crushed again. But this time, I didn't cry. I listened.

My husband is wise. All who know him agree upon this description of him. He is not one who will demoralize or demean you into changing. He patiently waits until you are ready. And when you ask, he offers suggestions that will change your life if you are willing.

He said, "A PERSON HAS TO RESOLVE TO NEVER LOSE CONTROL OF HER EMOTIONS AT ANY TIME WITH ANYONE."

By this time, I was deep in thought. What would this look like? What would this mean to my life and my relationships? What would have to change? Could I make the necessary changes?

Of this I was sure: To attempt this level of emotional control would be very difficult. It would take great humility. It would take an equal amount of courage. It would take incredible resolve, as my husband intimated. Was I willing?

I excused myself from the breakfast table.

I walked ten steps to my backyard, my outside haven. It is the little corner of my world where I retreat almost every day to journal. At the same time, it is the place where I find hope and enthusiasm, forgiveness and purpose.

In the quietness of that next hour, I replayed the week once again, in the presence of a holy God who surely desired a different, better way for me.

During those sixty minutes, the challenge my husband laid out grew into a purposeful conviction that I *could* resolve never to lose control of my emotions at any time with anyone . . . with God's help . . . should I decide to do so.

During that hour, another thought was impressed upon me: *How will people know that I have made such an all-encompassing decision?*

I must let them know.

How?

I decided to send a letter of amends and apologize to anyone I had hurt with my out-of-control emotions.

At first, only five people came to mind.

But within the next few days, I made a list of twenty-five people. I proceeded to send or e-mail the following letter to each of them on July 2, 2000:

Dear . . .

I hope this letter finds you and your family celebrating the summer with as much rest and recreation as work.

You are one of several persons whom I know and love, and yet

I know that I have hurt with my out-of-control emotions.

I would like to ask you to forgive me for the one or many times that I have hurt you with my sins of pride, uncontrolled anger, harsh words, and for being demanding and unappreciative. I am truly sorry that I have hurt or disappointed you—and God—with and because of my actions and words.

After seeking counsel on how I might truly change the above areas of my life, I was given a suggestion that I believe will change how I relate to everyone in my personal and professional life. I have decided to never indulge in out-of-control emotions and uncontrolled anger with anyone at any time. This is a huge step for me, but when I considered that I have been able to overcome alcoholism and abstain from alcohol for over twenty-two years, I knew that I could do this as well, with God's help.

If you are willing to accept my apology, you do not need to respond to this letter—I will see it in your eyes the next time I see you! But if there is any other way I have hurt you, I would ask you to e-mail me with the specific incident, hurt, or concern that might still be unresolved in your heart or mind, so that I might have the opportunity to ask you to forgive me for that, as well.

Sincerely,

Becky Tirabassi

Of the twenty-five people who received this letter, no one sent me a list of additional concerns that required further apology. Many recipients sent me very kind and encouraging letters, accepting my apology.

A few weeks after sending my letter, I attended a meeting at the home of a woman who had previously worked for me for only six weeks—which should tell you something. When I stepped into her foyer, she caught my eye and blinked. I thought it was a rather strange greeting, but I waved. From across the living room, she drew closer to me, never releasing me from a very intense gaze and fluttering eyelids. I finally had to say, "Cheri, what's up?"

She said, "My eyes, it's in my eyes!" She wanted me to see, know, and feel that her forgiveness was complete.

But my journey toward taming my temperament has not been without a few relapses. In fact, I remember each of them! I am most tested by airline employees, business associates, and while golfing with my mother.

Three years after making this resolve, I exchanged a few quick, fiery e-mails with a business associate who ended his last response with, "And as for your method of bulldozing, I am personally offended by it." This was a man who had previously received one of my "amends" letters. I held my breath as I re-read that line. Without even speaking out loud, I had offended him by demanding my way rather than by communicating with him in a professional manner until we could find a win-win solution.

I was once again caught and exposed as a person with an inability to control my anger. I immediately recognized the same painful feelings I had felt when I self-destructed in front of my employees during the house remodel. I was humiliated, regretful, and ashamed of myself.

BUT THIS TIME, I KNEW EXACTLY WHAT I NEEDED TO DO TO KEEP MOVING FORWARD INSTEAD OF RETREATING. While I wasn't proud to say I'd been here before, I used the painful—yet powerful—memory of my past experience to quickly rebound and resolve the situation.

I called my associate to apologize by phone and then sent a letter to him, restating my resolve to control my emotions and expressing my humiliation over falling short. I offered to meet him in person if he felt that was necessary. His response was simple: "I appreciate your spirit," he replied. "I forgive you."

Taming My Temperament

I have quite a feisty personality, both exciting and explosive. For years, people probably described me as a "time bomb" ready to wipe out anything or anyone in the vicinity. But I am also known as fun, bubbly, and optimistic. Because my personality is a blend of both playful and mover-and-shaker qualities, there are certain areas in my life that can spin easily out of control if not understood and watched. Money, sex, drugs, alcohol, food, and anger are areas that at one time or another have caused me very serious trouble.

Once I started learning about my specific personality, I made great advances in improving my relationships, as well as understanding my tendencies to procrastinate, lose things (including my temper!), and be disorganized. Compensating with fun and laughter only lasts for so long before the weaknesses catch up to you and you have to decide whether you will permit them to keep holding you back or whether you will figure out how to navigate through them. My ability to change and achieve goals and dreams was propelled when I understood the role of my personality.

Go with the Flo

In the late 1980s, I attended a speakers-training class held by best-selling author Florence Littauer. I walked in ready to simply learn the secret formula for writing and delivering powerful speeches. I figured I'd get my tidy little three-point outline in order and listen to Florence teach us how to deliver our key points for dramatic effect. Then I expected to leave, fully prepared to wow any crowd. Nice, simple, and easy.

But then came the curveball. Before any lesson, before any secrets, before any critiquing of our skills, Florence sat us all down and made us take a personality test. She was adamant that our passions and personalities were vital to understanding our communication style. Our ability to reach the audience had everything to do with the way we thought and acted even when we weren't on a platform.

The same is true for you. Your interaction with the world and your ability to get what you want, accomplish your goals, demonstrate your love for others, and make a difference in your own life and the lives of those around you are connected to how you're wired.

Do you love to have fun?

Are you a natural-born leader?

Do you love to be organized?

Are you a peacemaker?

Each question is a reflection of the different characteristics of the four personality types: Sanguine (Popular), Choleric (Powerful), Melancholy (Perfect), and Phlegmatic (Peaceful).

To help you understand more about your personality type, the same test I took under Florence Littauer's direction, "Your Personality Profile," is printed for you in Appendix A at the back of this book. I invite you to take some time to identify your unique personality. Here is an overview of each personality, reprinted with permission from "Your Personality Profile."

POPULAR SANGUINE

"Let's do it the fun way."
Desire: have fun

Emotional needs: attention, affection, approval, acceptance

Key strengths: ability to talk about anything at any time at any place, bubbling personality, optimism, sense of humor, storytelling ability, enjoyment of people

Key weaknesses: disorganized, can't remember details or names, exaggerates, not serious about anything, trusts others to do the work, too gullible and naive

Get depressed when: life is no fun and no one seems to love them

Are afraid of: being unpopular or bored, having to live by the clock, having to keep a record of money spent

Like people who: listen and laugh, praise and approve

Dislike people who: criticize, don't respond to their humor, don't think they are cute

Are valuable in work for: colorful creativity, optimism, light touch, cheering up others, entertaining

Could improve if they: got organized, didn't talk so much, learned to tell time

As leaders they: excite, persuade, and inspire others; exude charm and entertain; are forgetful and poor on follow-through

Tend to marry: Perfect Melancholies who are sensitive and serious but whom they quickly tire of having to cheer up and by whom they soon tire of being made to feel inadequate or stupid

Reaction to stress: leave the scene, go shopping, find a fun group, create excuses, blame others

Recognized by their: constant talking, loud volume, bright eyes

POWERFUL CHOLERIC

"Let's do it my way."

Desire: have control

Emotional needs: sense of obedience, appreciation for accomplishments, credit for ability

Key strengths: ability to take charge of anything instantly and to make quick, correct judgments

Key weaknesses: too bossy, domineering, autocratic, insensitive, impatient, unwilling to delegate or give credit to others

Get depressed when: life is out of control and people won't do things their way

Are afraid of: losing control of anything (e.g., losing a job, not being promoted, becoming seriously ill, having a rebellious child or an unsupportive mate)

Like people who: are supportive and submissive, see things their way, cooperate quickly, let them take credit

Dislike people who: are lazy and not interested in working constantly, buck their authority, become independent, aren't loyal

Are valuable in work because they: can accomplish more than anyone else in a shorter time, are usually right

Could improve if they: allowed others to make decisions, delegated authority, became more patient, didn't expect everyone to produce as they do

As leaders they have: a natural feel for being in charge, a quick sense of what will work, a sincere belief in their ability to achieve, a potential to overwhelm less aggressive people

Tend to marry: Peaceful Phlegmatics who will quietly obey and not buck their authority but who never accomplish enough or get excited over their projects

Reaction to stress: tighten control, work harder, exercise more, get rid of the offender

Recognized by their: fast-moving approach, quick grab for control, self-confidence, and their restless and overpowering attitude

PERFECT MELANCHOLY

"Let's do it the right way."

Desire: have it right

Emotional needs: sense of stability, space, silence, and sensitivity, support

Key strengths: ability to organize and set long-range goals, have high standards and ideals, analyze deeply

Key weaknesses: easily depressed, too much time on preparation, too focused on details, remember negatives, suspicious of others

Get depressed when: life is out of order, standards aren't met, and no one seems to care

Are afraid of: no one understanding how they really feel, making a mistake, having to compromise standards

Like people who: are serious, intellectual, deep, and will carry on a sensible conversation

Dislike people who: are lightweights, forgetful, late, disorganized, superficial, prevaricating, and unpredictable

Are valuable in work for: sense of detail, love of analysis, follow-through, high standards of performance, compassion for the hurting

Could improve if they: didn't take life quite so seriously, didn't insist that others be perfectionists

As leaders they: organize well, are sensitive to people's feelings, have deep creativity, want quality performance

Tend to marry: Popular Sanguines for their outgoing personality and social skills but whom they soon attempt to quiet and get on a schedule

Reaction to stress: withdraw, get lost in a book, become depressed, give up, recount their problems

Recognized by their: serious and sensitive nature, well-mannered approach, self-deprecating comments, meticulous and well-groomed looks

PEACEFUL PHLEGMATIC

"Let's do it the easy way."

Desire: avoid conflict, keep peace

Emotional needs: sense of respect, feeling of worth, understanding, emotional support

Key strengths: balance, even disposition, dry sense of humor, pleasing personality

Key weaknesses: lack of decisiveness, enthusiasm, and energy; a hidden will of iron

Get depressed when: life is full of conflict, they have to face a personal confrontation, no one wants to help, the buck stops with them

Are afraid of: having to deal with a major personal problem, being left holding the bag, making major changes

Like people who: will make decisions for them, will recognize their strengths, will not ignore them, will give them respect

Dislike people who: are too pushy, too loud, and expect too much of them. Are valuable in work because they mediate between contentious people and objectively solve problems

Could improve if they: set goals and became self-motivated, were willing to do more and move faster than expected, could face their own problems as well as they handle those of others

As leaders they: keep calm, cool, and collected; don't make impulsive decisions; are well-liked and inoffensive; won't cause trouble; don't often come up with brilliant new ideas

Tend to marry: Powerful Cholerics who are strong and decisive, but by whom they soon tire of being pushed around and looked down upon

Reaction to stress: hide from it, watch TV, eat, tune out life

Recognized by their: calm approach, relaxed posture (sitting or leaning when possible)

By now, I hope you recognize your personality blend of strengths and weaknesses, and I bet you can even identify the traits of your closest family members and friends. But before you get to finger pointing or criticizing their weaknesses, remember, each personality trait (including your own) has an equal number of weaknesses. The point isn't to say to yourself or others, "See, I knew you were stubborn, a procrastinator, gullible, or bossy." Instead, see the areas that are potential hazards for you and begin understanding how remaining unaware of them can hurt your relationships. That old phrase "Knowledge is power" is the key here.

In the beginning of this chapter, I suggested that *just about everything you do* is influenced by your personality traits. Almost invariably, the parts of yourself or your circumstances that you long to change correlate directly with your personality.

Now that you have taken the personality test and scored yourself, let's go through the list of activities I listed at the beginning of the chapter and see how personality affects the ways you may struggle or succeed in each of these areas.

EXERCISE . . .

If you look closely at the personality types, you can easily pick out which personalities probably enjoy exercise more than the other personalities and may even be avid athletes all their lives.

Populars: Need to find fun exercises—usually involving others.

Powerfuls: Like to find people to compete against.

Perfects: Often enjoy exercising alone.

Peacefuls: Often need people to force them.

In my family, I have a lot of my mother's genes. At eighty-one, she plays golf three or four times a week, regularly breaking 100. She has golfed for sixty years! She is full of energy and very athletic. We are very alike in this area, but more significantly, it means that I find it natural to be active and athletic.

If exercise is an area of life that you struggle to improve or change, and especially if being active or athletic isn't natural for you, you will have to constantly (probably all of your life) incorporate activities, such as group dance classes or hiking alone, that spark your interests or cater to your personality type.

How do you currently deal with exercise? If this is an area you cannot seem to change for good, what is something that you have learned about your personality that might make a difference in how you approach this? What is something you must tame about your temperament if you are going to have control in this area for your lifetime? _____

_____

_____

_____

ANGER . . .

Popular and Powerful personalities are much more susceptible to angry outbursts than are Perfect or Peaceful people.

Without going into great detail, among my two siblings and me, two are passive in expressing their anger and one is explosive. Any guess who the fiery one is? Though we had the same parents, my blend of personality traits (which are the exact opposite of my two siblings') deals explosively with anger unless it is kept under control—just one of the reasons I've had to write so many amends letters!

Because anger has been a recurring issue in my life for many years, for me to gain permanent control in this area I have to focus *daily* on strengthening this weaknesses in my personality. The most significant reason I am willing to keep it in check is because I know it can negatively affect other areas of my life. When I realized I was hurting people I loved and hindering my professional aspirations, I got serious about controlling my anger.

How do you currently deal with anger? If this is an area you cannot seem to change for good, what is something you have learned about your personality that might make a difference in how you approach this? What is something you must tame about your temperament if you are going to have control in this area for your lifetime? _____

_____

_____

_____

STUDY . . .

If you have children, it is important to identify and recognize your and your children's personality similarities and differences. If studying or learning is more difficult for your child, it might have something to do with his or her personality.

For people with personalities that are easily distracted (the Popular), it should come as no surprise that these personalities will struggle with sitting still for any length of time to study or read. If you recognize this trait in yourself or your child, it is best to find solutions, programs, and tools that help overcome those weaknesses.

When my son, a Popular Sanguine child, was in junior high, many of the parents in my neighborhood bought a popular set of audiotapes called *Where There's a Will There's an A*. We bought the tapes too, hoping they would help our son turn a corner in his academic life. Of course, after listening to the entire tape series, my son's only "catch" from it was this: "Every ten minutes children should take a study break"!

When it comes to learning and studying, Perfects find it much easier to maintain focus; they even enjoy time management! Powerfuls work best when there is a reward, and the Populars are often easily sidetracked or distracted if there is anything more fun to do. Of course, the Peacefuls are rarely in a hurry. They'll "get there when they get there"!

How do you currently deal with studying, reading, or learning? If this is an area you cannot seem to change for good, what is something you have learned about your personality that might make a difference in how you approach this? If applicable, what is something you must tame about your temperament in order to have control in this area for your lifetime? _____

_____

_____

_____

COMMUNICATE . . .

At work or at home, Perfects and Peacefuls tend to withdraw and isolate. They must work extremely hard to confront or apologize. Populars and Powerfuls must work just as hard not to attack. If you or someone close to you is trying to reach a goal, fulfill a dream, or overcome an obstacle, an effective communicator who speaks the truth in love will create an atmosphere where advice and feedback can be helpful rather than hurtful.

How do you communicate? If this is an area that you are working to improve (or someone close to you has suggested that you improve), what is something you have learned about your personality that might make a difference in how you approach this? What is something you must tame about your temperament in order to have control in this area for your lifetime?

_____

_____

_____

_____

SHOP . . .

Last weekend, my husband, brother, and a friend—each with very different temperaments—went shopping. As a Popular, my husband wanted it to be fun, so he had each person choose a store where each wanted to go. Roger chose the sporting goods store. The friend, a Powerful personality, chose the bookstore. And my brother, the Peaceful, happily tagged along with the other two.

Sometimes simply allowing for personality *differences* in others is the best way to progress toward your goals without getting sidetracked or being critical.

How do you shop? If this is an area in which you are different than someone close to you, what is something you have learned about your personality that might make a difference in how you approach this? What is something you must tame about your temperament in order to have control in this area for your lifetime? _____

_____
_____
_____

EAT . . .

Because the subject of health and fitness is such a hot topic, whether you are a struggler or want to help someone else who struggles to get eating habits under permanent control, it is important to be aware of the differing personality strengths and weaknesses that impact this area.

If you need to avoid hanging out with certain people because they are more impulsive with food choices than you can afford to be, then you must set limits and draw lines.

If you are a friend or family member of someone who is struggling in this area, take into consideration your differing personality traits and avoid being judgmental or tempting.

How do you deal with food? Populars and Peacefuls often struggle much more with discipline here. Powerfuls and Perfects find it easier to say no.

If this is an area you cannot seem to change for good, what is something you have learned about your personality that might make a difference in how you approach this? If applicable, what is something you must tame about your temperament in order to have control in this area for your lifetime? _____

_____

_____

PARENT . . .

It is a wonderful, wonderful asset to know your children's personality traits, especially when your Popular child loses his keys and cell phone for the tenth time! How can you get angry when he gets those very tendencies from you?! Finding solutions to improve or strengthen weaknesses for you and your kids results in permanent change rather than repeated failure.

If applicable, how does your personality play out in your style of parenting? How is your personality different than each of your children's personalities? What is something you have learned about your personality that might make a difference in how you approach this? What is something you must tame about your temperament in order to control this area for a lifetime?

_____

_____

_____

ORGANIZE . . .

This one is so obvious! Perfects love detail and order. Populars have no idea even where to begin to organize their rooms or desks. Powerfuls get someone to do it for them. And Peacefuls get it done at a snail's pace.

If you are in a leadership position and do not inherently possess organizational traits, surround yourself with people who do! Or if you desire to fulfill a dream and cannot seem to finish a project, you need to acquire resources, tools, and gadgets that help you, as well as strengthen this area of your life. Learn shortcuts, tricks, and tips from those who are organized. Those who desire to transform any area of their lives need a plan. In order to implement that plan, you have to bring organization into your life. If this is a weakness, figure out a way to harness your temperament and get the support and help you need.

How does your personality play out in your ability to organize? What is something you have learned about your personality that might make a difference in how you approach this? What is something you must tame about your temperament if you are going to have control in this area for your lifetime? _____

_____

_____

_____

_____

OVERCOME OBSTACLES . . .

The dreamer or visionary with Powerful traits will more fiercely fight and less easily give up than other personality traits. Therefore, if you know that your personality is more fearful or intimidated, you will need extra motivation and support to achieve your goals.

Two things are true: Every personality trait deals with obstacles in a different manner. And every person has to overcome obstacles. Recognize your weaknesses and strategize ways to compensate for them.

How does your personality overcome obstacles? What is something you have learned about your personality that might make a difference in how you approach current or future obstacles? What is something you must tame about your temperament in order to have control in this area for your lifetime?

_____

_____

_____

_____

_____

_____

In the introduction of this book, you were asked to list your dream, goal, or struggle in which you long to see breakthrough. As you consider your personality traits, what are ways you believe they are hindering your journey to improve your life?

What are areas in which you struggle that may have something to do with your personality? _____

_____

_____

_____

_____

_____

Brainstorm a couple of ways you might use your understanding of your personality to find a new solution or different approach. _____

_____

_____

_____

_____

How are the personalities of those around you playing into your desires to change your life? _____

_____

_____

_____

_____

How might the personality *strengths* of those around you help you? _____

_____

_____

_____

_____

What relationship(s) in your life would be improved if you made an effort to allow for personality differences? _____

_____

_____

_____

_____

What can you do to build up the strengths of the person or people listed above? _____

_____

_____

_____

_____

_____

_____

_____

four

Protect Your Mind

Our thought lives have the incredible power to either move us forward or hold us back from overcoming our addictions, improving our relationships, fulfilling our dreams, and reaching our goals. The mind may be a person's greatest vulnerability because it is so very, very difficult to diligently protect against the negativity, doubt, and criticism coming at us from all directions.

The fight to control your thoughts is different than simply driving out lies and focusing on the truth, as we discussed in the first chapter. Our moment-by-moment thoughts are even more susceptible to corruption than the big-picture truths because we are constantly barraged with images, opinions, memories, encounters, and conversations that flood us with ideas—both our own and those of others.

How you process and control those thoughts directly affects your ability to make and keep changes in your life. Do you pay attention to the combative voices (yours or others') that say you're in over your head, out of your league, and doomed to fail? Do you tend to entertain the prickly doom-sayers and invite them to come on in and make themselves at home? What does it take to kick the negative thoughts out, no matter how loudly they protest, fight, or even sweetly seduce you?

What all strugglers or dreamers must realize is that their situations, temptations, even their family members may not change, but their thought patterns are something they *can* control. Thoughts entertained by a person wanting to overcome procrastination, infidelity, financial irresponsibility, unforgiveness, anger, criticism, overeating, smoking, or any other challenge have great power to either propel that person forward or keep him or her in a rut.

We spent the last chapter exploring personality types and weaknesses. That knowledge is extremely helpful in understanding the mind battles you are prone to wage. For procrastinators to experience permanent transformation, they must daily fight off the tendency to give in to paralyzing fears, retreat into laziness, and especially, not succumb to the deadly game of rationalization.

Angry people must expect that every day they will be frustrated by something, have their buttons pushed, be disappointed by someone, or experience other numerous situations where their anger might flare. Opportunities for anger will never end. Therefore those who are committed to gaining control over their emotions, especially their temper, must always guard against the old, destructive thought patterns and replace them with new ones. The result will be noticeable, changed behavior.

Critical people will repeatedly face situations where they

have opportunities to judge or criticize someone. Instead, they must toss out the old way of thinking and commit to new thoughts.

Overeaters will always have food in their lives! They must learn to live with it by embracing new thoughts about food. From my personal research and experience, the real battle is won when people change the way they think about food. By lowering the importance of food in their lives from something they *love* to something they *need* for fuel or energy, they can immediately change their behavior. Success is possible when overeaters acknowledge from the beginning that they must valiantly wage a battle in their mind every day for the rest of their life.

Smokers have a similar experience. They will always see other people smoking and be in numerous situations that trigger cravings for cigarettes. Ex-smokers must always be ready to fight off fond thoughts about smoking with factual, healthy reasons why they cannot and will not smoke another cigarette.

In every instance, entertaining or allowing tempting thoughts to filter through and dwell in your mind during the beginning, middle, or end of your journey is terribly destructive to your resolve. The thoughts will come back daily, weekly, and monthly to see if they can haunt the one trying to achieve permanent transformation. And though the power of those thoughts is greatly diminished with every consecutive dismissal, there is never a time to feel overconfident. There are too many relapse stories to suggest otherwise.

Mind Games

As an alcoholic who drank herself to oblivion during a five-year span, I am intensely familiar with the mind games of a person who knowingly risks sanity, job security, and even survival because of an utter inability to stop using the very thing destroying her life.

I know it may be hard for an observer to understand, but in my particular situation, it wasn't long before my evening and weekend social drinking consumed more and more of my days and weeks. At the same time, and what appears to be of considerable consequence, my mind became consumed with very desperate, even suicidal thoughts. I tried pushing away the overwhelming guilt and regret for the things I knowingly and unknowingly did while drinking, but unless my every waking hour was eased by alcohol, these escapades weighed heavy on my mind. Yet I was too afraid to stop drinking because I knew no other way to live. It was a vicious cycle of giving in to my addiction in order to compensate for my out-of-control life.

Right before I hit the wall, I felt like I was barely hanging on to life. I imagined that ending it all would finally let me slip into an unknown place that was certainly better than what I had going. Still, I quietly hoped for a different, sober life. But I had no clue how to get there.

The inevitable fall came. I landed hard. And there was no recourse except to finally face my fear and admit I was an alcoholic. Though I was ashamed of the label, I could not deny that my alcohol consumption was the center of all the problems hindering me in my workplace, relationships, and emotions. In addition, this one behavior was clearly accompanied by other problematic behaviors (smoking, swearing, lying, cheating on my boyfriend). If I could just get a handle on the main stumbling block, I instinctively believed it would improve every area of my life. But my mind wasn't helping me.

The decision to quit drinking was my own. No one had to tell me my life would be better if I didn't drink, though more than a few people tried. Unfortunately, I never listened to sober voices. I WAS STUBBORN AND HAD TO LOSE EVERYTHING BEFORE I WAS WILLING TO SEE THE LINK BETWEEN MY UNHAPPY LIFE AND MY BEHAVIOR.

For alcoholics, the decision to quit drinking is often triggered by a crisis and takes a huge effort. It requires a concession of so much pride—beginning with the admission that others are right. It means giving up something you have grown to love and need. Addicts contend with tremendous physical with-drawals, and especially in the beginning days of abstinence, they must fight an all-out battle in their minds.

Some call my abrupt abstinence a "white light" experience. And though many take a longer time to make a decision *never to drink*, the mind is still constantly flooded with powerful thoughts that beg for a drink. Strangely, the parade of persuasive thoughts running through the mind sounds like good buddies nagging you to reverse your decision of abstinence and indulge *just one more time.* Those friendly, boisterous voices make sinister appeals, speaking lies such as, *You aren't really an alcoholic. No one will ever know if you have one drink. You can't be happy without a drink.* Or, *Why don't you quit drinking tomorrow?*

I CLEARLY REMEMBER HOW I OVERCAME THOSE THOUGHTS DURING THE FIRST FEW MONTHS OF SOBRIETY. AT THE SUGGESTION OF A WISE FRIEND, I REPEATED A SERIES OF NEW THOUGHTS EVERY TIME I CONSIDERED HAVING A DRINK. I spoke silently to myself, or sometimes even out loud, saying, "Get out of here. You are trying to kill me. You are poison. I'm not going back there. I'm not giving up my dreams, integrity, and newfound joy. I don't want to be a drunk. I want a new life." I also asked God to help me fight the battle in my mind. I was certain something very real was trying to steal my resolve.

To refrain from having one drink, even taking one sip, I *continually* held on to the thoughts that reflected my deepest desires. It was a daily, sometimes hourly, battle. I slowly gained strength in an area where I was previously weak. I had to antici- pate the negative thoughts, be ready for them, and expect them to come.

This was totally exhausting in the early stages. It was like being on a boat that was taking in water just as quickly as I bailed it out. Relaxing or letting up even for a moment meant the flood of negative thoughts quickly gained the upper hand and threatened to sink me. I had to immediately use my mind in order to hold on to the truth. What was the truth? I wanted happiness, self-respect, and a meaningful life *more* than I wanted to be high. Yet, in the beginning days of sobriety, I admit that a sober, happy life seemed more impossible than possible.

During the first few months of abstinence, the mind wonders, *Will I really make it?* Every day you realize how vulnerable you are, how often you must fight, how much easier it is to give in. Yet hours eventually turn into days of sobriety, and the storm of negative thoughts lightens up a little. In time, you can begin regaining control of other areas of your life. After only a few weeks, you actually feel better, think more clearly, and enjoy life so much more. After months, you have more courage and strength. After years, you have a deeper resolve that cannot be penetrated by those old thoughts.

But even though your thoughts, desires, and behavior have absolutely changed, a recovered alcoholic knows that no matter how many years of sobriety they possess, they can never let down the guard to their mind—ever.

At any moment, there might be a compelling thought, an unexpected opportunity, or even an old friend who reenters your life and perhaps unintentionally invites you to return to the old behavior. To break through to consecutive *years* of sobriety, you must stay guarded and keep your head in the battle—one thought at a time—one day at a time—for the rest of your life.

Invasion of the ANTs

The brain is the seat of feelings and behavior. Everything begins and ends in the brain. —Dr. Daniel Amen

My husband, Roger, recently attended one of Dr. Daniel G. Amen's seminars. Amen is a clinical neuroscientist and the author of *Change Your Brain, Change Your Life.* Roger spent an entire day listening to Dr. Amen show and describe brain scans of alcoholics, smokers, and others with brain-related problems. By the time Roger came home, he said, "Becky, you could be a poster child for this doctor!"

Roger was amazed at how Dr. Amen's scientific findings substantiated one of the reasons I believe I have abstained from alcohol and drugs for over twenty-five years without the help of medicine or therapy. Dr. Amen says that even a brain saturated and destroyed by chemicals can experience behavioral changes through the practice of controlling and managing thoughts.

In his books and seminars, Dr. Amen explains how every thought you have sends an electrical signal to your brain that can be recorded, analyzed, and visualized on a nuclear brain scan. He concludes, therefore, that our thoughts possess physical properties and are therefore tangibly *real*. He writes, "Teaching yourself to control and direct your thoughts in a positive way is one of the most effective ways to feel better."

Dr. Amen goes into greater detail when he shows his patients how their moment-by-moment thought patterns can be controlled through a series of steps they can master on their own. He strongly suggests that ALLOWING CRITICAL, BLAMING, CONDEMNING, ANXIOUS THOUGHTS TO RUN RAMPANT IN YOUR BRAIN IS SIMPLY POLLUTING YOUR BODY. He says, "Every cell in your body is affected by every thought you have."

In fact, he refers to negative thoughts and patterns as ANTs, or automatic negative thoughts. He not only encourages you to "talk back" to the ANTs but to understand that these thoughts don't always tell the truth! He suggests they even lie to you!

Interesting, isn't it?

While reading Dr. Amen's book, I not only found his whole concept *very* intriguing, but actually quite confirming of my personal experience.

In my early days as a recovering alcoholic in 1976, I tried describing to others what my battle against alcoholism, withdrawal, and suicidal moments felt like before I became sober. Amazingly, I told people, "It felt like I had ants crawling in my head that I couldn't reach and I couldn't get rid of."

For over two decades, whenever I shared my nonclinical testimonial of how negative, destructive thoughts overloaded my brain and almost sent me into a suicidal spin, I was actually describing what Dr. Amen calls *reality*! My thought patterns were so powerful and possessive and REAL that they almost talked me into ending my life. That close encounter was the morning of August 26, 1976.

By the afternoon of August 26, 1976, my life changed when I began talking back to those ANTs and telling them to leave! Though they put up a huge fight and did not want to leave, they eventually did—one at a time.

For those who are not nearly as desperate as a suicidal person but struggle with negative thoughts on any level, it is critical to see how fatalistic, depressing thoughts have the power to altar your mood, take away your joy, and encourage an overall cynical, complaining, pessimistic way of life.

Negative, destructive thoughts can ultimately convince you to give up, give in to temptation, or not care about the consequences of relapse. In essence, these thought patterns and habits are strong enough to keep you from sustaining the changes you so deeply desire, if you let them!

What I am asking you to do is take a radical approach to permanent transformation. IDENTIFY AND GET RID OF YOUR NEGATIVE THOUGHTS, ONE AT A TIME, EVERY HOUR OF EVERY DAY for the rest of your life.

If you feel uncomfortable with this idea because it sounds unorthodox, strange, or unfamiliar, then consider Dr. Amen's advice to "talk back" to your negative thoughts, write them down to expose them for what they are, and replace them with positive, affirming thoughts! Seeing the ANTs in writing may give you courage to see them for what they are and actively go after them.

FEAR FACTOR

Negative thoughts have just one goal as they burrow their way into our heads. They want to make us afraid. If we are scared, we will stay where we are or possibly even shrink back from ever reaching our potential and making a difference in this world. A fearful person sacrifices productivity and effectiveness—and for what? A safe life? What good is that when you come to the end of your life with nothing to show for it? The thought, *Well, at least I didn't get hurt*, will be of little or no comfort when you are asked to describe what could have been.

Fear is . . .

► refusing to get help because you make up your mind that people will judge you.

► dwelling on the words of a single critic even though ten other people tell you they believe in you.

► believing the voices that tell you it was a mistake to take a risk.

► listening to the urgings telling you to turn back and give up.

The result of fear is unfulfilled dreams, failed resolve, broken relationships, missed opportunities, unkept promises, relapses, and ultimately, a squandered life. This is the ammunition you must use in talking back to your negative thoughts. Are you truly willing to give them power over you to rob you of fulfillment, progress, and joy? If not, tell them to get out!

It may be helpful in determining the source of your fears to frequently refer back to the principles in chapter 1 that led you to identify the lies you believe. Many of the fearful thoughts you have are the direct result of false beliefs. If you fail to remain diligent in your watch over them, they can quickly get the upper hand.

In keeping with Dr. Amen's analogy, I picture those old cartoons that show an army of ants raiding a picnic gathering. They are persistent, clever, and daring in their attempts to steal food. Left unnoticed, they end up carrying off huge sandwiches, cakes, and watermelons—ruining the picnic!

The impact of fear in our lives is one of the most destructive forces with which we contend. NEGATIVE THOUGHTS AND THE FEAR THEY PRODUCE WILL STEAL EVERY GOOD THING IN YOUR LIFE—including your joy, your hope, your courage, your faith, and your potential.

But you are not helpless to defend against the ravages of fear. You don't need to search hidden passageways, dark corners, or under rugs to find fearful thoughts and proactively attack them. In fact, I can tell you right now where fear is born, bred, and comfortably thrives: in your thought life! Fear is nurtured by the internal and external voices that cause you to doubt your purpose, passion, and promises.

SWIMMING WITH THE SHARKS

In 1984, I became a sole proprietor and started a small company from a home office. I began speaking at hundreds of events in almost all fifty states, and I wrote numerous books that each incorporated the phrase *Change Your Life* in the title. It was a powerful and familiar phrase that succinctly captured my mission.

In the summer of 1996, I decided it was time to reassess my life and its course. I set aside forty days to deeply consider the next decade of my life. I reflected, analyzed, prioritized, read, journaled, and prayed.

At the end of forty days, I spent an entire afternoon sifting through the ideas that had developed during that time. I narrowed my thoughts into a comprehensive business strategy that incorporated my existing speaking and writing pursuits into the media of television and the Internet.

I called my idea Change Your Life.

Shortly after this forty-day planning period, I took small measures to expand my passion to "change people's lives for the better" from a regional to a more national level. My first step was asking a neighbor, a lawyer, if he knew anything about trademarks. It wasn't his area of expertise, but he graciously (and freely) helped me locate the forms to register Change

Your Life. Then he kindly reviewed my application and advised that I create a Change Your Life logo to include with my submission.

By the end of 1997, I received the trademark Becky Tirabassi Change Your Life®, Inc. for publishing, events, and media purposes. Immediately, another young entrepreneurial friend designed an edgy website for me, allowing me to instantly reach thousands of people with my balanced-life message. Change Your Life had a place and a face—potentially—in every American home by way of the Internet!

My dream was finally taking shape. Though still very small, Change Your Life was a multimedia company making a positive difference in America through publishing, live events, and the Internet.

Still, I knew my greatest desire—and challenge—was taking my message to national television. Though I appeared as a guest on many cable and regional television shows, I could not find an open door to any of the network or national outlets.

During this time I managed to acquire (I think I begged) a literary agent at one of the top three talent agencies in the country to represent me. Though we pitched my idea to numerous publishers, it was not until 1998 that a contract was secured for the book *Change Your Life*.

I sincerely believed that signing with a New York publisher was all I needed in order to launch Change Your Life onto television. So I asked my literary agent to set up a meeting for me with the television department of the agency.

I felt fortunate—and excited—about the meeting! With great enthusiasm and a clear vision (in my mind) of the impact that Change Your Life could and should have through television, I drove up to Los Angeles in the spring of 1999. I truly expected everyone I was about to meet would love and embrace my idea without reservation!

I arrived right on time, full of enthusiastic optimism. After waiting in the lobby for at least thirty minutes, I was led to a conference room and given a seat at a huge, round, empty table and again asked to wait. Alone in this large room, I felt very . . . little. But I was still full of passion for Change Your Life and certain I could convince others of its powerful, life-changing message.

As each agent came into the room, he or she seemingly possessed a power that intimidated and unsettled me. I quickly felt insecure and insignificant.

It probably wasn't as brutal as my mind remembers, but the last ten minutes still play out in slow motion. Beginning with my lack of experience, one by one, the agents explained exactly why I was unqualified for representation by their agency. And perhaps because I didn't appear to understand, someone finally said, "Becky, you don't even have a clip reel with one national television appearance for us to see you delivering your message on camera!"

I recall feeling as if I was a stranded swimmer in the middle of the ocean surrounded by a ring of sharks. Each took a big bite of me then left me bloody and for dead. And then the meeting ended.

As each agent quickly shook my hand before leaving the room, I remember telling myself, *Just don't cry. You cannot cry.*

I—and my dream—took a pummeling.

Along with some of the agents who were in the meeting, I rode the slow elevator down to the lobby. I got off and walked to my car, almost breathless.

I had plans to meet a friend (who was a publicist) for an early dinner after the meeting. Of course, I had made the original plans with the anticipation of giving her *all* the exciting details of my meeting. Now I could hardly imagine how to describe the horror of this meeting without enduring another round of devastating humiliation.

At the core of my pain was a terrifying thought: *What does this mean for Change Your Life?* These people had the power to help me break into television, but they did not embrace— much less even see—my vision for taking Change Your Life to a television audience. They did not agree with me that women in America were looking for practical ways and personable role models to help them balance their lives physically, emotionally, spiritually, and mentally.

Perhaps the worst part was the thought that it wasn't just my idea they rejected. In essence, they rejected me. They did not believe I had any level of talent or potential that made it worth their time to invest in me. In so many words, they basically said I'd never accomplish my dreams.

On the way to dinner, I still didn't cry, but I felt physically ill. The overriding emotion was shame. I had no idea what to do next, and it seemed quite reasonable to consider simply giving up.

My publicist friend expressed genuine sympathy upon hearing my version of the agent meeting. And perhaps out of pity, but to her credit, she said, "Becky, there is a national cable show taped in Los Angeles on which I regularly book guests. I am sure I can get you on that show within a few weeks. We'll get you a reel. Besides, just because those agents didn't capture your vision doesn't mean it isn't a good idea or that you won't change lives!"

On the long drive home that night, my thoughts vacillated between *You are nothing and nobody* to . . . *I will not, cannot, give up.*

THE MOST CRITICAL CHOICE I MADE BEFORE PULLING INTO MY DRIVEWAY WAS DECIDING WHICH THOUGHTS I WOULD FOLLOW. Nothing but discouragement and criticism was poured into me at that meeting, but now I had to decide if those voices would guide my actions from that moment forward.

I truly only had one choice. Even though I was completely humiliated, I could not base my future on one meeting. Even though I met with smart, powerful people, I would not let that deter me from finding a place on television where I could encourage people of all ages to change their lives for the better!

I shoved out the criticism and doubt and pushed forward.

On April 28, 1999, true to her word, my publicist friend booked me on the Paxnet show called (at that time) *Great Day America*. I was as nervous as I was thrilled for my first live, national television appearance. I had a blast sharing my story and the *Change Your Life Daily Journal*, my self-published balanced-life resource. And for everyone to forever witness on my reel, the host ended the interview with, "Becky, you're a good speaker!"

As I left the studio, I made another crucial decision to dwell on his words. And I pressed on, *with a clip reel*, looking for more opportunities to take the Change Your Life message to network television.

I did not have another breakthrough until November 2000. I was a guest on the nationally syndicated talk show *Men Are from Mars, Women Are from Venus*, hosted by Cybill Shepherd. Because it was taped in Los Angeles, many of my friends and family were in the studio audience to encourage me!

Also seated in the audience was a producer from a network morning talk show. Ironically, when this young producer was in high school, she had heard me speak at a large youth convention. After the taping, she approached me and affirmed my enthusiastic presentation of the Change Your Life message delivered in front of both a live and television audience. A few weeks later she pitched me as a guest for her show, and her bosses loved the idea!

By January 2002, my first national network television

appearance resulted in twenty-seven additional appearances on network television, including a ten-week guest contributor series on the *CBS Early Show* during the summer of 2001 called "Change Your Life with Becky Tirabassi™." In that series, almost three million television viewers—every week—received both inspirational hope and practical ideas for changing and balancing every area of their lives.

As I write this, this story feels very incomplete. I almost didn't even include it because the truth is, my dream of taking Change Your Life to a daily platform on network television is only partially fulfilled. I wish I had the full storybook ending to share, but I don't. Not yet, anyway. . .

This is the part of *Keep the Change* in which I desperately hoped to tell you my dream was fulfilled, the door has opened, and I've broken through. But my book deadline is here, and there is no open door as of yet. I still have only my faith, hope, and a dream to hold.

Of course, my pitching and telling the story has never stopped. Though I grow fatigued at times, ashamed of my slow progress, and hit with waves of discouragement with every rejection letter or call, I can't seem to give up this dream.

All along I've been thinking that the greatest encouragement I could offer would come from a success story, not a lack of achievement!

This brings me to being truthful with you regarding one of my current struggles: I fight thoughts of feeling ashamed that

I haven't achieved my goal and feeling rejected and like a failure. Here is how it works in my life: I'm doing fine, even in the day-to-day struggles, until . . .

I read or see something that makes me feel jealous, or . . .

I take a close look at my company's bank balance, or . . .

I get passed over for something I know I could do if just given the chance.

Within minutes, I plummet. I start to drown, get anxious, or frustrated with something or someone. My thoughts move from hope-filled to obsessive. My focus gets blurred, my thinking less clear. I procrastinate . . . and I'm hindered.

I know what I must do right then. What I've done every other time—protect my mind and get rid of the ANTs. I must face my fears and fight them off. I am fighting and winning the battle of my thoughts by daily telling the truth, letting the pain push me forward and harnessing my strengths. I can promise you that my dreams and determination are bigger than the daggers my negative thoughts may throw at me.

Radical Thinking Leads to Radical Living!

Positive thinking is not a novel or revolutionary idea. It is a concept heralded by every helping profession as the place in each person's life where the battle for control is waged.

Whether you want to . . .

> lose weight or inches,
>
> drop your cholesterol count,
>
> be an "on time" person,
>
> quit smoking,
>
> heal a relationship,
>
> get organized,
>
> stop yelling, or
>
> start a new career . . .

you must learn to identify, kick out, and replace every negative thought that enters your mind.

Whether you have a long or short road ahead of . . .

> physical therapy,
>
> restoring your marriage,
>
> improving your character, or
>
> rebuilding a bankrupt savings account,

holding on to lasting change in your life will happen in this order: one thought then one action, one day at a time.

As you attempt to *keep* any change in your life—consistently controlling the thoughts that enter your mind *must* become a daily habit.

SQUASH THE ANTS

No matter how large or small the dream, achievement, or struggle . . . if you will view it as a battle that is won first—in your mind—one thought at a time, you can begin having victory today.

Start by resisting negative, critical words that pass through your mind. Be sure to recognize them. Identify them for what they are: distractive, disrupting, or deceitful lies that have the power to demean, destroy, or disillusion you.

Forget wallowing in the pain or injustice of how they got there and just tell them to leave. In the end, it doesn't matter if they were taught or spoken. Realize that you have the power to dismiss them by either shooing them away or ignoring them as quickly as they come.

Equally important, always replace negative thoughts with positive thoughts. Positive thoughts are just as powerful to encourage you and move you toward your goal as negative thoughts are to deter or even destroy you. DO WHATEVER IT TAKES TO STOP THE INVASION OF THE ANTS! Speak out loud to yourself—shout if you must! Write down your positive thoughts and read them often. Carry around an inspiring quote in your pocket that you can pull out whenever necessary. Figure out a personal plan of attack for the next time you are tempted to listen to the destructive voices.

What is a common thought that holds you back, makes you fearful, tempts you to give up, or feeds you with negativity?

_____

_____

_____

_____

_____

_____

How do you think the thought is harming you? _____

_____

_____

_____

_____

_____

In writing, tell the thought it is no longer welcome in your mind. _____

_____

_____

_____

_____

Replace the thought with words that encourage, affirm, and inspire you. Talk to yourself as you would talk to a close friend who is struggling with negative thoughts. _____

_____

_____

_____

_____

_____

_____

Write down a quote, verse, or saying that is particularly inspiring to you. _____

_____

_____

_____

_____

_____

_____

What would a fearless life look like for you? What would you do, accomplish, or change? _____

_____

_____

_____

_____

Write a fearless statement of commitment to drown out the negative voices and reach your goals. _____

_____

_____

_____

_____

_____

_____

_____

_____

_____

_____

_____

_____

_____

_____

_____

_____

_____

_____

_____

_____

_____

_____

_____

Develop a Strategy

At the beginning stages of change, you might experience numerous euphoric highs and even feel a few exciting surges of positive movement toward your goal. You may start feeling invincible, expectant that your journey will be easy.

It is only a matter of time before your resolve begins fading as signs of difficulty or unexpected temptations rudely interrupt your momentum.

You falter. Your confidence is shaken.

At this juncture, you may realize that the change you so deeply desire will require more than blasts of emotion, heartfelt desire, or wishful thinking. You are faced with the undeniable reality that permanent transformation demands a developed strategy. It will take a bold strategy to keep your body, mind, spirit, and emotions all moving simultaneously in an unfamiliar, new direction!

Like any mission statement or business plan, noble intentions are meaningless unless a powerful strategy produces visible results in the details of your life. Your life should look different to yourself and those around you. Your strategy must include a lifestyle change. If you think you can change your life without changing your life*style*, you only set yourself up for failure.

In the book *Changing for Good*, authors James Prochaska, John Norcross, and Carlo Diclemente suggest, "Difficult as it is, forsaking an undesirable behavior is not enough to overcome it for good. Almost all negative habits essentially become our friends—even, in many cases, our lovers. To overcome them fully, we must replace our problem behaviors with a new, healthier lifestyle."

One Day at a Time

In the introduction of this book, I asked you to imagine you were heading out on a trip and could never return to your life as you left it. Sounds a little extreme, but here's what I meant.

To develop a strategy for lasting change, it will require a balance of discipline and enjoyment that powerfully engages your body, emotions, spirit, and mind in new, healthy patterns and behaviors. We've talked a lot about breaking the habits of mind, personality, and emotions. Now I want to move into the daily strategy.

You can think about, hope, and plan for change and achievement all you want, but until you're able to put one foot in front of the other, one day after another, you'll never have success. Your ability to sustain lifelong breakthrough increases exponentially if the places you go, the people with whom you interact, and the activities in which you participate begin to change one day at a time.

SURRENDER THE OLD

Begin the new strategy with surrender. Though it's easy to muster initial enthusiasm over the *concept* of a healthy lifestyle, the *reality* requires more than envisioning that new life. In order to fully possess and live it, the first step is stripping away and shaking off the affection toward your former life . . . and bravely embracing a new one.

You must surrender your old ways. You must develop a new way. You must develop a strategy to find enjoyment with new activities, healthy relationships, security, and purpose.

I assure you, the surrender of the old ways and embracing the new ways can be very motivating and captivating. In fact, I encourage you to focus often on the benefits of the exchange. YOU ARE TRADING SORROW FOR JOY. YOU ARE EXCHANGING LIES FOR TRUTH. YOU ARE SWAPPING THE BAD FOR THE GOOD, WRONG FOR THE RIGHT. You are bartering fake for authentic. You are giving up old and used for something new and better. You are losing in order to gain.

Yet the struggle to control an unruly body, emotions, or thoughts in order to overcome weaknesses, establish new habits, or reach impossible dreams can no longer remain a battle in the mind but must be accomplished by tangible behavior changes.

You must surrender yourself to discipline. Elton Trueblood, in his book *The New Man for Our Time*, wrote, "When we begin to ask what the conditions of inner renewal are, we receive essentially the same answers from nearly all of those whom we have most reason to respect. One major answer is the emphasis on discipline. In the conduct of one's own life it is soon obvious, as many have learned the hard way, that empty freedom is a snare and a delusion."

He continues, "Excellence comes at a price, and one of the major pieces is that of inner control. The one who would like to be an athlete, but who is unwilling to discipline his body by regular exercise and abstinence, is not free to excel on the field or the track."

Many of us resist discipline. Whether it is simply foreign to our lifestyle or repulsive to our nature, changing the way we run our daily lives is extremely difficult. But if you desire to achieve change in any part of yourself, the external details of life must be part of the process.

So as you said good-bye to comfort and familiarity a few chapters ago, understand this is the best trade-off you'll ever make. If you need to go from an all-to-nothing or from an always-to-never change you must take one action, one day at time. It is the only way to turn out-of-control behavior into a controlled, healthy lifestyle.

The good news is that changed behavior is not forever elusive. You absolutely do not have to give in to relapse or repeated failure. If you will develop a plan that allows you to experience small achievement, you will begin to see, feel, and experience lasting change in brief, then in accumulative ways. No one, not even the most successful person, instantly gains consecutive days of new behavior. Everyone must build hours into days, months, and years of healthy patterns. Permanent change cannot be bought in advance, but it can be attained through a practical strategy and transformation of daily life as you know it.

DRAW UP A WRITTEN PLAN

Physical and behavioral changes, when aided by a concise, structured plan or contract, give us the daily, moment-by-moment guidelines we need to eat right, exercise regularly, abstain from specific temptations, or reach personal goals. Putting form to the vision makes all the difference.

I am asking you to set limits or draw lines for your life that are visible, not vague or unrealistic. YOU NEED A WRITTEN STRATEGY FOR EVERY AREA OF YOUR LIFE. I suggest that you do not leave it up to your own imagination to change your behavior.

You might begin by calling a personal board meeting consisting of a small group or team of family, friends, or supporters and asking them to help you develop a strategy. Some of you will sit and do this with a counselor or life coach. If you are really fighting for this change and cannot seem to break through, this could make all the difference.

The goal is to begin by brainstorming a variety of tangible possibilities and behavior changes. Write down all the ideas; be open to consider every idea as a good idea. Be willing to incorporate the *proven* ideas of those who have achieved past and present success in the area on which you are working.

The goal of the team will be to develop an actual written contract based on six questions that define your strategy and is signed and witnessed by those who can hold you accountable. As people who are regularly a part of your life watch your progress, you can get their feedback. If you keep your need for change hidden or quiet and try to change on your own, you miss out on a lot of opportunity for encouragement and possibly even slow yourself down.

Give your team permission to check on your progress in regular increments. In severe cases of backward movement, you might even give them permission to call an intervention!

For those who struggle with emotional issues such as jealousy or bitterness, writing a "letter of admission and apology" that includes your methods for change allows others to see that you are aware of an area of your life that needs to improve . . . and asks them to help you keep the change! Even spiritual growth goals can be charted out in specific terms.

The routines you create need to include entertainment,

work, exercise, hobbies, and education that are supportive and not destructive to the changes you are making.

There is an incredibly simple way to untangle the complexities involved in both minor and major behavioral change. THE WRITTEN PLAN FOR EVERY STRUGGLE, GOAL, OR DREAM IS TO ANSWER SIX QUESTIONS: WHY? WHAT? WHEN? WHERE? WHO? AND HOW? If you are diligent to answer honestly, you will have a strategy that expresses your mission, vision, and values in a tangible plan.

WHY?

Why is one of the most powerful questions you will ever ask yourself:

- ► Why am I willing to change?
- ► Why do I want to change?
- ► Why do I need to change?

This is a question about what ultimately motivates you. Without a motivation that goes deeper than your urges, temptations and weaknesses, you'll never be able to counter the deadly question, Why not . . . ?

Why not just one more time?

Why not start tomorrow?

Why not give up?

Why not go back to the way things were?

You will have to take a look at the relationships, situations, temptations, workplace, and living environment that make up the details of your life. Whatever caused you to stumble or give up in the past will continue as a threat unless you are willing to dramatically stake out limits, restrictions, new behaviors, and boundaries. Until then, you will never feel like the space within the newly designed framework is a true haven of rest and safety for you.

As simple as this may sound, I believe the answer to the *why* question comes when you allow love to enter into your experience.

Let me suggest that ONE OF THE DEEPEST MOTIVATIONS TO CHANGE AND KEEP THE CHANGE IS TO EXPRESS AND EXPERIENCE DEEPER LOVE: love for others, love for God, love for yourself.

For people who struggle in significant relationships such as marriage and parenting, the answer to, Why do I, will I, should I . . . ? gives you reason and motive for being . . .

faithful
patient
merciful
forgiving
honorable
respectful, and
trustworthy.

Understanding the answer to *why*, for me, always begins when I ask, "Why am I bothering when it's so hard and I'd rather quit?" The answer I get is, "Because of love."

The first time I asked the question, "Why should I change?" it led me on a search for truth and purpose. My *why* question begged me to be transparent and honest in going beyond myself. It led me to a stunning discovery that I was loved and that God had a purpose for me. That discovery sustained me for twenty-five years. Why am I sober? Because I am loved and so that I can love others. And why will I stay sober? Because I am loved and so that I can love others.

When I ask *why*, I always find myself considering how to love others in ways beyond my abilities. The *whys* allow me to exhibit mercy and grace in all the other areas of life.

The answer to *why* I should let go of what is bad or wrong, I believe, is found in love. As I am loved, I, in turn, can exhibit love for another, myself, God . . .

Why do I love, even though I might get hurt?

Why do I trust, even when discouraged?

Why do I forgive others?

Why do I stay committed?

My core beliefs allow me to go beyond myself, to change my life for the better.

The power of love in your life, as a form of motivation, is the one piece you can never leave out.

What, When, and Where . . . ?

The answers to *what, when,* and *where* have the potential to create a huge wave of inner resistance. The inability to give specific answers to these questions in the past might be the very reason you have experienced no significant progress toward change in your life to date. Hesitating, delaying, or never answering these questions can keep permanent transformation at bay.

Answers to *what, when,* and *where* give definition to your old behavior, commitment to your new behavior, and a reason to look to your future. They represent the most basic details of your resolve.

► *What* must I do to change?

► *When* do I need to adjust my daily schedule to keep the change?

► *Where* do I need to go (or not go) to give me the best chance at success?

Giving honest answers to these questions will undoubtedly redefine or even restrict your present freedoms. Yet, hold on to the certainty that you are heading down a path to a more authentic freedom that will absolutely and positively change your behavior and your life!

Look more closely at the first question of *what*. It's a simple identifying statement that pinpoints the problem, the challenge, the dream, or the hurdle. You can't reach a goal until you know what the goal is. Until you determine *what* you must do differently today, tomorrow, and the next day . . . lasting transformation will remain elusive.

When and *where* often go hand in hand. For a struggler to overcome, the *when* and *where* in their daily lives must be filled with healthy substitutes, new activities, and new locations in order to achieve lasting change. Begin with identifying the *whens* and *wheres* that frequently got you in trouble before.

Maybe you are tempted to buy junk food when you walk down the ice cream aisle at the grocery store. Or maybe you struggle with feelings of comparison or failure when you read the alumni update that highlights former classmates who seem to be curing cancer, ending hunger, and brokering world peace! Those are exaggerated examples, but give this real thought. Consider in your life the times when the temptation to give up or cut a corner is the most persistent. How can you counter those moments and protect your resolve with a diversion or healthier way of spending the time?

The law of cause and effect is at work in the *whens* of your life. Decide when you are most vulnerable to discouragement and determine to bring in whatever reinforcement is necessary to keep yourself afloat.

If you knew someone with a gambling problem, the first place you would tell him to avoid is the casinos, right? As obvious as it seems, changing where you spend time can be pivotal to staking out new ground in your process of growth.

Ask yourself *where* you tend to encounter the most temptation or feel particularly susceptible to those nagging ANTs. For the alcoholic it might be a nightclub or, for the overspender, a shopping mall. Part of planning out the parameters of a new life will involve identifying these places and figuring out alternatives. Maybe you can suggest meeting your friends at a coffee shop instead of a bar. Or you might decide that a day with the girls is better spent at the lake than the mall.

The answers to *what*, *when*, and *where* clearly define a new set of actions for those who struggle. If you'll take time to consider how they apply to you, I am certain you'll begin to see real solutions for holding on to your resolve.

WHO?

The next questions you must answer are

► *Who* can help me in this process?

► *Who* is hurting my journey toward lasting change?

Before you build a new life, you must make absolutely sure you're building on a rock-solid foundation made of trust, commitment, purpose, and strength.

On our very first day of marriage, I had an alcohol relapse after a year of sobriety. That day I asked my husband if he would never drink with me for the rest of our lives. I knew for me to succeed in sobriety, I needed to have someone with whom to never drink, and I needed to make sure there wasn't alcohol within reach. He agreed, and we made a decision to never have alcohol in our home.

Since returning from our honeymoon twenty-five years ago, we have never had alcohol in our home on any occasion with anyone at any time. I have never had a drink, never relapsed, and never even wanted a drink . . . and I always have someone with whom to share a toast of water when everyone else is enjoying champagne at a wedding. That decision provided me a safe barrier that shielded me from my temptation to drink.

If you have a great desire to hold on to a change you have made in a specific area of your life, it is imperative that you surround yourself with people who . . .

> ► speak affirming, encouraging words into your life,

> ► clearly understand your goals and can help you reach them,

> ► model the life you want to live, and

> ► will be loving and honest with you!

You can never have too many encouragers, but even one discouraging word or tempting person can set you back. You must drown out the voices that try to bring you down, take you back, or steal your resolve; instead seek out people who offer you safety and strength.

For children and students, these people can be parents, school counselors, teachers, bosses, and mentors. As we become adults, we expand our sphere of influence: spouses, coworkers, personal trainers, doctors, counselors, siblings, and friends. For addicts, there are free and voluntary programs in almost every city or region that offer peer counselors, sponsors, and pastoral staff who provide necessary programs and personal accountability to help you keep your desired changes.

Here are a few more words of caution:

1. I receive many calls and letters from people who say they do not have or cannot find support or accountability. Keep looking. If one particular counselor or group doesn't click with you, then look for another one! They are out there.

2. Inevitably, if you are counting on one person as your constant source of hope, encouragement, and nurture—and that person doesn't follow through—your tendency will be to get discouraged or even feel resentful. Be sure to enlist many willing supporters who provide encouragement and support in both physical and emotional ways.

3. Use the telephone. The moment you struggle, as soon as you feel overwhelmed, or the instant you sense fear filling your mind . . . that is the very minute you need to pick up the phone and call a friend, mentor, sponsor, pastor, or whomever you can trust to "talk you down off the ledge." If the thought to make the call comes into your mind, act on it. That is exactly why these people are on your team—to support you physically, emotionally, and spiritually.

4. Finally, on those days when you don't feel like holding on, when your courage to abstain is waning, your hope takes a hit, or your faith is fettered by fear . . . it is extremely motivating

to know that someone you admire or respect is hoping, rooting, and pulling for you to succeed. On those days, someone else's expectations of and for you may be the only reason you maintain unhindered progress toward your goals.

With a great willingness, you must surround yourself with people who have similar goals and lifestyles to those you want to embrace.

At the very same time, after you have identified your support team, you must also identify specific friends or acquaintances or coworkers who deter you from personal growth, healthy choices, or achieving your goals. You must have a strategy for breaking off, separating, distancing, and/or setting up healthy boundaries with them. This is definitely a place where many people who want lasting change get stuck and even reverse direction. But this is a nonnegotiable component if you truly desire long-term success.

It is not even enough to simply identify an unhealthy relationship. You must set limits and draw lines that have firm boundaries. Always having an escape plan, or role-playing a conversation of what you would do if unexpectedly confronted with negativity, insensitivity, or temptation, is essential to avoid losing ground.

In case for any reason you missed this, hear me again: Letting go of unhealthy relationships with friends, acquaintances, or coworkers is a nonnegotiable option in a powerful strategy for permanent success.

HOW?

The last question supplies the words-to-action step:

> ► *How* can I achieve lasting transformation in my life?

The answer will come as you gather your supporters, look over your strategy, consider the *whys, whats, whens, wheres,* and *whos* . . . and then turn your commitment into action. You will likely find that the answer to the *how* question is simply, "One day at a time." The final stage of *how* takes your good intentions and nudges you out the door, where you will begin living a changed life . . . not just dreaming of one.

The Journey from Why? . . . to How?

Let's look at ways these questions and stages fit together to answer the *how* in a few specific incidents.

ADDICTION

The *why* in the life of an addict can be complex. I do not represent myself as a psychologist, but I think a common theme with addicts is the sense of being unloved. Finding lasting motivation for change may involve uncovering a series of lies centered around thoughts of being unlovable. However, once addicts can see the truth and understand the depth to which they are loved by God and those around them, they are more empowered to stop filling the void with all the wrong things.

Also, this acknowledgment of being loved frees a person to demonstrate love to others. A parent may come to a place of finding motivation to stop drinking out of enormous love for his or her kids. In answering the question, "Why is it worth it to me to keep this change?" the most powerful motivator will be focused on love.

What must an addict do to change? As simple as it sounds, an alcoholic must stop consuming alcohol. Alcoholics cannot ever drink alcohol, and addicts can never use if they desire to transform their lives permanently, which in their case is sobriety.

You would be amazed—truly, truly amazed—at how long addicts will wait before saying the words, "I will/can never use." They will deny and rationalize the power that alcohol has over their lives, delaying permanent change, often until a crisis erupts.

Yet answering, "What must I do to change?" often involves a second step. What they will exchange or substitute in place of the alcohol is just as important for an addict to determine. Though sparkling and mineral waters, coffee, tea, and sodas are healthier, nonalcoholic choices, they do not have the kick, or the high, of an alcoholic drink. As for smokers or drug addicts, temporary solutions such as nicotine chewing gums do not replace the activity. The fact that no substitute is a healthy one means that EVERY AREA OF AN ADDICT'S LIFE MUST BE ENGAGED IN HIS OR HER BEHAVIOR CHANGE.

Incorporating social activity, counseling sessions, group meetings, or even exercise must be considered as you continue to answer what in your life.

The next question is just as important.

When do alcoholics need to be on guard against temptation? In the case of addicts, the answer to the *when* question gives them a very specific strategy. Once again, they must acknowledge when they are most vulnerable to drinking and create diversions or alternate ways to spend their time. If someone struggling with abstinence drank alcohol after work, on weekends, on certain occasions, or at special events, these times must be protected with new uses of those times.

Especially for the addict, the *where* even more fully defines borders. For example, my father, who was a blue-collar worker and an alcoholic until the age of fifty-five, always stopped at a bar for a few beers on his way home from work. After a stroke, his doctors told him he could never drink again or he would die. He was given only one option. His lifestyle and behavior had to immediately change.

Instead of going to a bar, he went to a local coffee shop where a number of men sat at a counter—at the same time every day—and had a few cups of coffee. That activity simply replaced *what*, *when*, and *where* he drank with different, better behavior.

Others might have to attend regular meetings for alcoholics in the evenings, after work, or especially during those times when they used to drink. Eventually, recovered alcoholics will attend weddings but never toast with champagne, find different weekend activities to replace nightclubbing, and even decide if they will keep or serve liquor in their homes.

The answer to *who*, especially for an addict, is a huge component in recovery and sobriety. *Who* can very often be determined by before and after, new and old. Upon making a decision to abstain, the friends, colleagues, and acquaintances with whom you associated before you made the decision to quit are most likely those with whom you will have to set limits. This boundary is very, very, very difficult. Young people tend to see this disassociation as losing friends and missing fun rather than gaining sobriety.

The answer to *how*, for one who desires sobriety, must be specific. In the case of recovering sex, drug, and alcohol addicts, a written daily plan that includes scheduled meetings, random checkups, and constant evaluations has become a proven path for millions. Loose or vague intentions, instead of a carefully designed strategy for changing your life for good, will keep you in a repeated cycle. Breaking out of self-defeating cycles happens with a strategy!

WATCH YOUR WEIGHT

Out-of-control eating is the plight of millions of men and women! And though there is a plethora of fads, diets, and plans available, the battle for control over this area of life rages in almost every American home.

I personally believe it is very, very possible to be an over-comer, or self-changer, in the area of food and fitness. It begins and ends with having a strategy.

Especially for people who struggle with food, an eating and exercise plan should be made daily and often reevaluated. A strategy for those with eating disorders *must* include predeter-mined, healthy food choices and food portions, and a support system of both sponsors and other sojourners.

Why? By answering the question *why*, you will sustain a commitment to becoming healthy and begin to reprogram the way you think about yourself, your body, and your worth to others. For example . . .

1. I like who I am.

2. I want to show love toward my family by providing nutri-tious meals.

3. My body gives me a chance to experience this life, and I want to treat it well.

4. The people in my life love me just as much now as they would if I were a size 4.

What? When? Where? In developing a list of specific new and healthy behaviors, it is important to identify the foods, portions, and behaviors that did not achieve long-term change.

In every case, just thinking about preparing long lists can keep people from moving toward a new lifestyle. Asking specific questions such as, "*What* foods are off limits? *When* do I eat poorly? *Where* do I most often lose control with food?" reveals the very things you must replace if you are going to sustain changed behavior.

Who? Because eating is a daily activity, the answer to *who*, in the case of an overeater, includes everyone! Family, friends, and coworkers will always be a part of our mealtimes. Explaining your strategy to them and asking them to help you are essential to your short- and long-term success.

For the one who struggles with food and weight issues, the answers to *why, what, where, when,* and *who* will provide you the solutions to *how* you can establish a new and healthy plan:

1. Plan your meals in advance and detail specific grocery-shopping items.

2. Schedule time on your calendar to plan meals, make grocery lists, and grocery shop.

3. Brainstorm ways to relieve anxiety: hot tea, bubble baths, walking with a friend, journaling.

PAST THE WISHING

The dreamer, as well, must identify a specific plan that will turn her big idea into small steps. Asking the same six questions will begin to give your dream shape and form.

Why can be quite cathartic and empowering as you reach into an amazing source of purpose and passion.

What is the dream in your heart?

The answers to *when* and *where* give the insights into how long it might take to achieve this dream or where you need to go for help or further education.

The answer to *who* can help will often provide an extensive list of mentors, sojourners and trailblazers. And the *how* can become the beginning of your business plan that will evolve over time.

Those with athletic, financial, or educational goals find that these six questions define daily action steps. With every answer, they move methodically toward their goals. The question, "*Why* do I want/need/have to do this?" often remains the guiding motivation during the toughest times. *What* do I want to achieve? *When* can I make necessary adjustments or create time to focus on this? and *Where* (what location) do I need to be in order to do this? *Who* can I ask to help me? And *how* allows me to turn my desires into visible, daily, tangible action steps.

I mentioned at the beginning of this book that there would be times along the way when I would ask you to do more than consider a radical approach to permanent transformation, but to embrace it. This is one of those times. For you to run toward a new life, I believe it is time for you to identify any misdirected affection you have toward that which is keeping you from the changes you desire. I am asking you to turn your back on them. I AM ASKING YOU TO MAKE A DECISION OF YOUR WILL, NOT OF YOUR EMOTION.

I am asking you to consider how you must think and speak and act in new ways, not just for today, or once in a while, but as daily or often as necessary.

I am asking you to purposefully let go of the wrong thought patterns, words, friends, and to stop going to those locations that keep you from experiencing lasting change, the achievement of your goal, or the fulfillment of your dream.

Take the time now, before you move forward, to ask yourself the six questions about an area of your life that you desire to change for good:

Why are you willing to change? _____

_____

_____

_____

_____

_____

_____

What are you trying to change/accomplish? _____

_____

_____

_____

_____

_____

_____

When do you need to adjust your daily schedule in order to help
you keep the change or take you further toward your goal?

_____
_____
_____
_____
_____
_____
_____

Where do you need to go (or not go) in order to give yourself
the best chance at success? _____

_____
_____
_____
_____
_____
_____
_____

Who can help you in this process? And who might be hurting
you? _____

_____
_____
_____
_____
_____
_____

How will you achieve lasting transformation in your life? (Write a detailed mission statement and game plan for winning this battle.) _____

_____

_____

_____

_____

_____

_____

_____

_____

_____

_____

_____

_____

_____

_____

_____

_____

_____

_____

_____

_____

_____

_____

_____

Capture Reality Daily

I must make a disclaimer at this point.

I have written at least three other books that encourage readers to keep a journal of their thoughts, feelings, goals, and prayers. In fact, I have designed two journals that have sold over three hundred thousand total copies, and for nineteen years I have filled countless journals of my own with records of my thoughts and feelings as well as my conversations with God.

If you have read any of those books, or use either of the journals, or adhere to the practice of journaling on a daily basis, or have heard me speak about journaling, *and you are convinced through practice* that journaling must be a lifelong habit for those who desire to experience permanent transformation, then you can skip this chapter.

But if you have not been able to *keep* change in your life—in a specific area or in many areas for any length of time—*and* you do not journal on a daily basis, this point in our journey is the time to make a nonnegotiable decision.

PUTTING IT ALL TOGETHER

So far, I have encouraged you to . . .

- ► tell yourself the truth
- ► harness your pain,
- ► tame your temperament,
- ► protect your mind, and
- ► have a strategy to change your behavior.

Now it's crunch time. As you begin to pull each of these components together, you need a place where they intersect and make sense in relation to each other. You will benefit tremendously if there is one constantly evolving document that lays out the pieces of your journey and evaluates them regularly.

A daily journal provides a tangible instrument through which you can record how you think, react, feel, and adjust to change to your life. When you give yourself a chance to sit down for just a few moments each day and assess where you have been, where you are, and where you're heading, you are able to keep up with yourself, in essence.

A daily review of your goals versus the reality of your day gives you an amazing chance to make small adjustments as you go. It is a time to chart small slips or giant leaps, or simply to record heartfelt emotion. And then you can determine what your next day must hold in order for you to stay the course.

If you do not set an appointment with yourself each day, it is unbelievably easy to get six months down the road and suddenly realize your passionate resolve to change your life got ditched about 180 degrees ago. Then getting back on track is so much more consuming and difficult than if you were to simply make the minor alterations each day.

Journals satisfy different needs for different people. Some folks use them to pour out their feelings in an almost cathartic release of emotions. Artists and creative types will jot, sketch, draw, or doodle. They take what is in their minds and put lines and shape to their thoughts. Others are much more analytical in their approach to journaling. They see it as an opportunity to plan, evaluate, and chart progress.

You should feel free to make your journal into whatever will help you stay focused and remind you how far you have come and why you are willing to keep going. For some, considering the *what, when, where, who, why,* and *how* questions in a checklist each and every day might be the very best way to stay on track. But if your preference is to simply write about how you feel, that can be equally important.

No matter your style, THE KEY TO EFFECTIVE JOURNALING IS TO SEE IT AS A VEHICLE THAT CAN TAKE YOU WHERE YOU WANT TO GO. However, until you get in and start the engine and step on the accelerator, an idle vehicle is wasted. The power source for the vehicle is honesty. You must honestly record the details of your day—the temptations you faced, the battles you fought, the victories you won, and even the tumbles you took.

Much of the time, the issues you journal about will represent ongoing plans, struggles, or commitments and will help bring them to a quicker resolve. For example, as you write in your journal about lies you believed (or still believe), you will begin processing them and become more aware of them. In the past, those lies could revolve in your mind, but journaling about them will cause your radar to identify them much more quickly.

When you develop a strategy for your business, personal health goals, or even abstinence, a written plan allows you to see it often, become more familiar with it, adjust it, and eventually know it well enough to articulate your strategy to others. This becomes helpful both as a source of prevention and direction.

As you lay out your long-term goals—or even a mission statement—in writing, your progress toward achieving those goals or mission will have stops and starts along the way. Journaling allows the accomplishment of small steps to give you an emotional lift, a sense of accomplishment on the way. A JOURNAL IS A TOOL TO USE IN THE WAR OF YOUR MIND AND BODY.

Especially while you are struggling to establish a new discipline in your life, journaling can be a very tangible record of both your desires and your accomplishments. Yet because journaling is an activity that requires consistency, if you can master it, it will carry over and have a positive effect on every area of your life you are working to improve. Journaling goes hand in hand with the new habits you are trying to acquire. It gives you the snapshot of your day's progress.

Write Your Story, Day by Day

If you are struggling to balance more than one area in your life, I encourage you to consider using a journal system that requires you capture *every* area of your life physically, emotionally, spiritually, and mentally—in writing.

Why do I encourage you to journal in all four areas of your life? Because how you feel emotionally will affect how you perform and feel physically, and where you are spiritually will affect what defines your purpose in every hour of your day. A journal gives you a place to see how intertwined these areas of your life really are. You will begin to make the connections between feelings and behaviors that may change the entire way you see your life!

ACHIEVE A HEALTHY BODY

If your battle is with food, exercise, or abstaining from an addiction that controls your body, you are one of millions of men and women who struggle to control their negative or harmful appetites and lusts.

Through daily journaling, you will definitively see if you are winning the war between your body and your mind. If not, you have the chance to catch yourself and bring in outside forces to help you keep your desired changes before things get too far out of hand!

Daily journaling gives you a pulse on your progress to change your unhealthy appetites and behaviors in light of your written and verbal commitments. A journal record of that promise or vow has the same effect as an audiotape or video recording. You can't deny that you wrote it. Of course, you can avoid it. You can procrastinate. You can try to squirm your way out of it . . . but a journal record is black-and-white proof of the truth. If your body is winning the battle over your heart, the inconsistency and broken promises will be a great reflection of your weaknesses. Which leads me to another reason why I encourage you to journal . . .

When I began to record the healthy foods I was going to eat each day and when I would exercise during the week, an immediate benefit occurred: a sense of order and peace came into those areas of my life. I no longer obsessed about food and exercise or alcohol when I had a specific plan for dealing with each of those areas.

A COMMON TRAIT OF STRUGGLERS IS THINKING TOO MUCH ABOUT THE OBJECT THAT HAS CONTROL OVER THEM. A journal has the ability to give strugglers a vital, visual component to reverse and then change their thinking. The more specific and practical the steps, the more the struggler experiences a regained sense of control!

For example, a written plan for eating right or exercising regularly takes the obsessive thinking out of the mix and provides a strategy for achieving your goals. A journal allows you to see that your goals were written when you were caring for your body, not abusing it. The more often you review your daily eating and exercise goals, check in, and keep it current, the sooner you will receive strength to make your body obey the written plan.

Ultimately, if your plan is realistic and designed with your age, environment, temperament, and desires in mind, the goals have a much greater chance of being achieved than if you did not keep a journal.

The beauty of a written strategy, determined at least one day in advance, is that healthy patterns are established at home, on the road, or even on vacation . . . and you're caught off guard less often. By planning in advance, you can visit the grocery store, call ahead for special meals, or even surf the Internet for eateries and places to work out when away from home.

After years of journaling about how I want to keep my body healthy, I find that I rarely divert from my healthy food choices. I am "programmed" to exercise three times a week. I have rarely missed that mark for well over ten years, and perhaps the best benefit of this journaling to support my physical goals is that I have weighed about the same for as long as I've written down a daily plan for eating right and exercising regularly.

An eating and exercise journal is both a goal and a record.

It doesn't do the work for you, but it sure helps you make sense of life when it starts feeling a bit too busy and over-whelming!

WRITING EXERCISES THE EMOTIONS

If you struggle to tame your temperament or strengthen specific character weaknesses, journaling is the place to lay it all out on the line and take a personal inventory.

Anyone can benefit from writing about thoughts, feelings, experiences, shortfalls, doubts, fears, anxieties, emotions, or regrets. If you have been hurt, your journaling can be a catalyst for extending forgiveness. If you have hurt someone else, it can be the impetus to ask for forgiveness. Or when emotions such as anxiety or anger get out of control, journaling is a very practical method for releasing that inner pressure.

In 1999, a study in the *Journal of the American Medical Association* reported that "confessional writing improved emotional and physical health." It added, "New research suggests that journaling is far more therapeutic than anyone ever knew." Researchers asserted that writing exercises can help alleviate symptoms of asthma and rheumatoid arthritis. Also in this JAMA study, results found that asthma patients who wrote about experiences such as car accidents, physical abuse, divorce, and sexuality improved their lung function by 19 percent. They found direct physiological evidence that "writing increased the level of disease fighting lymphocytes circulating in the blood stream and modest declines in blood pressure."

What should you write about? Start with your thoughts and your feelings.

Most of the time, when I am writing about my emotions, I find myself hammering out certain character flaws, trying to figure out how to deal with relational or financial concerns, or regretting something I did.

In a free-flowing journal, I let it flow!

The *Change Your Life Daily Journal* (see Appendix B for sample journal pages) focuses on two basic areas that bring healthy emotional balance into your life: forgiveness and giving. After all these years, not a day goes by in which a name or action step doesn't become clear when I ask myself these two questions during journaling: *Is there anyone I need to ask to forgive me or whom I need to forgive? Is there something I have that I can give to someone who needs it today?*

If you are either a spouse or parent, you have probably experienced significant challenges that require you to become less selfish and more giving or less judgmental and more forgiving.

Character flaws in your life will become more apparent the more you journal. Rather than run from them, take time daily to think on how you might improve them.

Another method for prompting you to get to the bottom of some of your emotions is to ask yourself questions that prompt healthy emotional release in your life. For example, *Why do I feel this anxiety? What could be causing these feelings of fear? Why did that comment hurt me so much?*

A journal that poses such questions to you on a daily basis—and leaves space for your answer—is a very powerful method for experiencing self-discovery and lasting change.

BALANCE IT ALL

Brian Dyson, CEO of Coca-Cola Enterprises from 1959 to 1994, said, "Imagine life as a game in which you are juggling five balls in the air. You name them—work, family, health, friends, and spirit—and you're keeping all of these in the air. You will soon understand that work is a rubber ball. If you drop it, it will bounce back. But the other four balls—family, health, friends, and spirit are made of glass. If you drop one of these, they will be irrevocably scuffed, marked, nicked, damaged, or even shattered. They will never be the same. You must understand that and strive for balance in your life."

Achieving balance in life is truly an art.

Our responsibilities overwhelm us; we've said yes too many times and not enough no's. And we come dangerously close to shattering our lives and the lives of those we love.

I often hear things like, "I don't have *time* to balance my life!" Between carpools, jobs, meals, diapers, business meetings, homework, housework, bills, telephone calls and sleep, you may be one of these people who think, *Who has time to change her life?*

I know it's hard to believe, but life was not designed to exhaust us. There comes a point when you have to sit down, take a breath, and get a grip on what you can and cannot do.

There is a hidden secret within this discipline of journaling. If you will take the time to do it, it will give time back to you in the form of a simpler, more organized, less hectic day. In the midst of your day, your goals and dreams will be forever recorded—never forgotten or discarded.

HOW WOULD YOUR LIFE CHANGE IF YOU RECORDED YOUR OBJECTIVES ON PAPER EVERY DAY? If you keep a to-do list, you are halfway there. But lists that are made are only effective if they are kept in a visible place, attached to something that won't get lost or disposed, and offer a method of checking off when completed.

Whether you are consistent at keeping an ongoing to-do list or you entered the twenty-first century living by electronic reminders, most agree that those who write down their daily agenda are more effective and efficient than those who do not.

For those of us who have big dreams, the benefit of a to-do list is the organization it brings to dividing a big dream into small, daily action steps. Visions and dreams remain wishes unless you can both see and experience forward movement. As you journal about where you want to go, the action steps tell you how to get there.

For those of us who want desperately to improve a relationship or who desire more effective communication at work or at home, written reminders and electronic organizers simply help us keep our commitments and promises.

I agree with W. Clement Stone: "If we fail to plan, we plan to fail." Being on time and prepared in advance are two powerful traits of an organized person. Therefore, if you are one of the personalities (Popular or Peaceful) who struggle more with organization than others, it is especially important for you to find *just the right* tools and resources that keep you moving toward your desired goals and unfulfilled dreams.

GROW YOUR SOUL

I regularly walk with my neighbor Jane. We only met about a month ago and really enjoy chatting and walking. As the deadline for this book grew near, I almost had to cancel our morning walk, thinking I should stay home to keep writing. But she didn't want to accept a cancellation and asked, "Is there any way I can help you?"

I said, "Actually, yes. I'm stuck on something. Would you mind if I brought over a chapter to you?"

She was so encouraging and said, "Please bring it along, and we'll talk about it."

I printed out this chapter . . . because that is where I was stuck.

As we started our walk, I gave her a little talk on each of the chapters, and then I mentioned how important I believed journaling is to achieving one's goals.

We talked quite a bit about writing down our physical goals, journaling about thoughts and feelings, and even making to-do lists, as well as the endless struggle to achieve our "to-do's." We were on the same page up to this point.

Then I began to tell her about the spiritual component of my journal.

She said, "Oh, you're going to lose a lot of people right here. People don't want to have God forced on them."

"I know," I replied.

She said, "People don't necessarily want religion. Or they simply don't believe in God, unless of course something terrible happens. Then they'll look for Him or let Him in."

"I know that, too, and that is why I don't want to lose people who are reading the book at this juncture."

We both laughed when I asked, "After we have this conversation, you'll keep walking with me, right?"

At the halfway point in our walk, Jane told me about a friend she used to walk with frequently. She said, "She would tell me about her day, and I would tell her of mine. Then we'd be honest with each other. If I didn't think she'd made a good decision, I'd tell her, and she'd tell me her thoughts as well."

At the end of our walk Jane asked with a smile, "What are you going to do about the God thing?"

I laughed and said, "I just have to be honest."

For me, writing down my conversations with God is as real as taking a walk with a friend. It is where I can be honest and say, "I'm stuck." It is the place where I receive advice. It is a real relationship in which I can be transparent. When I talk and listen to God, I am encouraged to pursue change in my life and keep it, rather than stay stuck.

So even if I might lose you, my reader, I still have to be honest with you.

But I hope you'll keep walking with me.

I am suggesting that you be open to including God in every area of your life by having a daily conversation with Him. I am the first to tell you that journaling will help you achieve your goals. But I have even stronger reasons to encourage you to do this. I've experienced permanent transformation in very significant areas of my life—and if that is what you are looking for, I am trying to show you a way that has worked for me.

What I have found is that I can stay connected and focused through writing. If I just close my eyes and pray, I fall asleep. If I try to sit still with eyes open and try to meditate, my mind wanders. PUTTING PENCIL TO PAPER TURNS MY THOUGHTS INTO RECORDED CONVERSATIONS. THEY REMIND ME THAT I AM NOT ALONE.

After more than nineteen years of writing my conversations with God, I receive a peace and confidence as I open my journal and turn to a fresh, clean, empty journal page. I also have come to believe that God speaks, directs, and helps those who are sincerely looking for Him and actively listening for Him.

If you are new to this idea or need a few ideas on how I do it, here are a few suggestions that have been thoroughly tested by hundreds of thousands of others over the centuries, including me!

COMMUNICATE HONESTLY

The simplest way I find to communicate with God is to approach it like any other conversation where I talk, as well as listen.

Both journals I designed include a "talk to God" and "listen to God" section. I find it important that my conversations are not one-sided.

While considering ways to journal, I have learned much from the guiding principles of those who have written on the subject, even though their words were penned decades or even centuries ago. C. S. Lewis, Mother Teresa, A. W. Tozer, Carlo Caretto, Henri J. M. Nouwen, and Peter and Catherine Marshall are just a few of the authors whose teaching has given me incredible insight.

In all of my research, the premise is this: Transparent conversations will transform your thinking, your appetites, and your weaknesses. Your vision will expand, your convictions will deepen, and your passions will inflame. If they are written, they become validation that He is powerful to hear, answer, and change our lives.

Initially, I remind you to COME TO EVERY CONVERSATION WITH GOD WITH THE KNOWLEDGE THAT HE LOVES YOU. This might take some doing. But when you realize that you can never earn God's love, and yet He still loves you because He *is* love, then you can begin to live your life, not out of guilt or penance, but out of gratitude and with purpose. Talking with Him becomes a sense of partnership in an adventure rather than a duty or a chore.

After a while, you will begin to see evidence of Him in your life. In many cases, you feel a presence, as if someone is walking with you. Eventually you cannot wait to sit down with pen and paper and express your thoughts, hopes, and dreams to Him, knowing you will be heard, advised, comforted, and even disciplined when necessary.

Mother Teresa said, "God has sent the Spirit of truth, he dwells in your heart. You have only to listen, to follow; and he will lead you to the complete truth. He leads you through all the events, all the circumstances of your life. Nothing in your life is so insignificant, so small, that God cannot be found at its center."

Your journal writing can be reflective, poetic, and insightful. It can be the cries of your heart penned with ink and stained by tears. It can be lines of random thoughts until something begins to clearly take over and you connect with God!

For centuries, men and women have talked with God with closed eyes. For me, by recording these conversations, I can keep my easily distracted mind more focused. By keeping lists of people for whom I am asking God to help or protect or divinely heal, I am much less likely to forget.

Because my life is full of urgent interruption in the form of e-mails or telephone calls and a myriad of other responsibilities, unless I make an appointment on my calendar to journal, it just won't happen.

In fact, I imagine that I am actually meeting with God. This very powerful picture reminds me that my appointment is not so much a diary or a rigid discipline of the physical and mental but also the spiritual.

I have found, as you will, that times of journaling will refine your character. If you are desperate for character cleansing and development, this is a most confidential, inexpensive arrangement in which to see your life change before your eyes.

Of course, the intensity and transparency of these conversations will often include desperate calls for help. George Muller, a man whose life is marked by leaving a great legacy of housing and feeding orphans during a desperate crisis in England, said, "My eye is not on the density of the fog, but on the living God who controls every circumstance of my life." The more he talked to God, the more he knew how He was going to work and act. Therefore, over time, when George recorded his requests, especially for the needs of the destitute, his conversations were impassioned and bold . . . and answered! The amazing written record of George Muller's life is indisputable proof that his God answered him, even when things looked impossible.

The practice of journaling can be therapeutic as much as enlightening; you will experience a new level of honesty with and about yourself when you stay with the discipline.

Because I have a propensity to spin out of control in every area of my life at a moment's notice, it becomes a lifesaver for me to daily take an inventory of these areas of my life *in the presence of God*. Henri Nouwen, author of numerous books on the inner life, in a written record of his admission to God said, "Why do I keep relating to You as one of my many relationships, instead of my only relationship in which all others are grounded? Why do I keep looking for popularity, respect from others, success, acclaim, and sensual pleasures? Why, Lord, is it so hard for me to make You the only one? Why do I keep hesitating to surrender myself totally to You?"

The journal-writing experience, when it includes these conversations, adds eternal perspective to every thought, dream, and request.

As if on a walk or out to coffee with a friend, I simply share my concerns, questions, and requests for others and myself, as well as thank, express awe, confess, and then listen—in writing.

CAPTURE YOUR CHANGE AND HOLD ON TO IT THROUGH JOURNALING!

In almost every case, the most concrete way to capture your daily thoughts and feelings is in writing—in keeping a journal.

A JOURNAL WILL RECORD HOW YOU ARE KEEPING THE CHANGE IN YOUR LIFE.

If you were to allow a camera crew to follow you around all day like they do in reality shows, you and all those who watch the replay of the tape would know how you are progressing in each area of your life. Most of us never want that type of accountability in our lives. If someone heard our every word or could see through us and hear our true motives, how might we live differently?

A journal asks you to replay *your* day in writing; it captures your daily reality.

Do you want to eat healthier and exercise more often, but you are exhausted and rush home to the couch, television, or even a cocktail to relax . . . and completely toss out the idea of stopping at the gym on the way home from work and then cooking a healthy meal?

Do you desperately want to make extra money but have found the effort of finding a part-time job that fits into your life paralyzes you, so you just let the wish fade away rather than search for a job?

Do you love someone but fear that any intimacy might push you from friendship into something more serious and you just can't go there . . . so you shut the door on something more?

Do you get so angry with family or coworkers that you blow up frequently but secretly regret your outbursts and wish you could change?

Do you procrastinate even to the point of losing an important opportunity, yet you long for victory over your personality weakness but just don't know where to begin?

A journal captures daily reality in your life.

IT'S ABOUT TIME

Keeping a journal is perhaps the most time-consuming aspect of this approach to keeping change in your life. It requires that you . . .

- ► focus inwardly,
- ► honestly evaluate all aspects of your life,
- ► admit faults or failures,
- ► hear the truth about yourself,
- ► express your emotions,
- ► distinguish lies from the truth,
- ► fight a battle against negative thoughts,
- ► think new thoughts, and
- ► make decisions.

Perhaps the greatest encouragement I can give you, the most practical advice you will find in this entire book, is this: IF YOU WANT TO PERMANENTLY AND POWERFULLY TRANSFORM ONE OR MANY AREAS OF YOUR LIFE, YOU MUST CARVE OUT A SPECIFIC AMOUNT OF TIME— DAILY—TO EVALUATE YOUR LIFE, YOUR GOALS, YOUR CHARACTER, AND YOUR RELATIONSHIPS. I do not consider this an option but an essential component in a radical approach toward achieving lasting change.

For a lot of people, the only feasible time to journal is in the morning before the household awakes, which may mean going to bed earlier the night before. You will have to schedule an appointment on your calendar to journal. It is important that the time you arrange is the most uninterrupted and productive time possible. Once you figure out when you'll do it, there are a few more considerations to help guarantee success.

First, I ask you to you consider journaling as a nonnegotiable commitment in your approach to permanent transformation. When I made this decision years ago, I gave myself no escape hatch and decided to make a commitment to journal for the rest of my life. To give yourself the best opportunity to see small and perhaps even substantial change in your life, I suggest that you make a minimum commitment to journal for at least sixty days.

Second, for your journal time to be consistent, it must be scheduled onto your calendar at least one day in advance (whether you decide to journal for fifteen minutes or sixty minutes).

I've given you a few ideas that work whether you are a man or a woman. But if these journal outlines or patterns do not work for you, buy an inexpensive spiral notebook or a beautifully bound leather journal, date the first page, and simply begin!

Of this I am sure: If you will commit to setting aside daily time to write down your thoughts, set goals, and record your

conversations with God, you will have black-and-white proof
that you are daily being changed, healed, and permanently
transformed. In fact, I encourage you to try the four sample
Change Your Life Daily Journal pages in the back of this book
(see Appendix B) as one method of journaling. However you
decide to do it, please make a decision (in writing!) about how
and when you will keep a daily written record of your life
before you move forward to the next chapter. _____

_____

_____

_____

_____

_____

_____

_____

_____

_____

_____

_____

_____

_____

_____

_____

_____

_____

_____

Gain New Perspective

What ultimately makes changing your life worth the struggle? When no one else thinks you can do it and your inner desires fight you all the way, what keeps you going? When nobody is watching, what keeps you accountable? To justify the cost of doing the work and enduring the pain, there must be a *reason* beyond yourself to fuel your passion.

Perspective describes the way you see your life, your situations, other people, and even your world. It's what gives motive and purpose to everything you do. Your perspective is wholly individual. No one else sees things exactly the way you do . . . because nobody sits where you sit or walks where you walk. It is influenced by thoughts, feelings, pasts, and experiences. It dictates your judgment calls and defines how you approach and engage the components and people in your life.

Embracing a New Perspective

In order to keep the change at every stage in your life, you will need to embrace a new perspective that will take you from . . .

- ► achievement to love,

- ► control to surrender,
- ► temporal to eternal,
- ► shame to sacrifice,
- ► promises made to promises kept, and
- ► desiring change to keeping the change.

In the narrow focus of a single hour, what you may see is a house full of screaming children, a stack of unpaid bills, a friend with cancer, a hostile boss, a corrupt system, or a broken marriage.

What would happen if you stepped back and saw this single hour from a different perspective? A perspective where your purpose and motivation are based on the knowledge that you are loved and in turn can show love? Suddenly you are willing to soothe the crying baby, let go of the stress over the bills, cherish the sick friend, forgive the hostile boss, work to fix the corrupt system, and heal the broken marriage.

In chapter 5, I asked you to determine *why* you are willing to change. If things like money, revenge, or pleasure are your motivation, you could have an impossibly difficult road ahead of you. But the minute you embrace a new perspective, everything can change . . . including you!

FROM ACHIEVEMENT TO LOVE

At one of my speaking engagements in South Carolina, a businessman named Lee Fogle was in the audience. Little did anyone know that he came to hear a Change Your Life message because he secretly knew he needed a significant transformation in his life and marriage.

To look at him, you would have thought he had everything a man could want: a beautiful wife, three kids, a gorgeous lakefront residence, sports cars, and vacation homes. But the Lee Fogle that no one saw was a man driven by an uncontrollable appetite for all the excesses that life offered.

I found his story so intriguing that we interviewed him during a segment I did on the *CBS Early Show* in 2001. In the interview he said, "When buying things and acquiring things and achieving success in business didn't satisfy and fill the hole, I sought happiness where I could find it."

His wife, Liz, was equally honest about the way their marriage had disintegrated due to his self-centeredness. She said, "Life was mainly all about him."

In the meantime, he drifted further and further from his family. His inability to value the people in his life over his need to succeed and acquire possessions caused him to almost lose what really mattered.

Lee was blind to the reality of his life and the consequences of his choices because his perspective was one of selfishness and destruction. Only when he finally stepped back and saw the big picture did his viewpoint change. It began with a startling discovery that he was both deeply ashamed of himself and humbly aware that in spite of his mistakes, God and his family forgave him. When he allowed forgiveness—the most gracious

and healing form of love that one can give or receive—to powerfully change his situation, he suddenly "saw" with new eyes.

Immediately he knew he needed a new road map for changing every area of his life, and he jumped into a daily journaling
plan. As a result, he became more and more transparent with
everyone about his behavior. Liz was the first to see the difference and acknowledge that he became "a better husband, a
better father, a better man."

M. Scott Peck determined that an achiever or overcomer has
the best chance to succeed if the motivation behind his attempt
at self-discipline is established in love. In his book *The Road
Less Traveled*, he wrote, "It follows, then, not only that self-
discipline is usually love translated into action, but also that
any genuine lover behave with self-discipline and any gen-
uinely loving relationship is a disciplined relationship." In other
words, if you cannot seem to force yourself to exhibit or
incorporate positive behavior, Peck might suggest you are
lacking the motivation of love—either for yourself or others.

Throughout his book, Peck firmly places the onus of true and
lasting change within the grasp of every individual. In revealing
case studies, he asserts that those who hold themselves responsible to others in conscientious, tangible, disciplined-out-of-love
behavior are those who experience and achieve personal and
lasting growth.

I am convinced that great power is released when you
embrace your life from a perspective of love. Like a camera's

wide-angle lens pulling back to reveal the whole picture, the moment you understand this concept of love, your battle for change is transformed. Your fear is calmed. Your pain is soothed. Your dreams are revealed. Your thoughts are renewed.

FROM CONTROL TO SURRENDER

It is painful to watch people make complete messes of their lives—especially when they admit to despicable and deceitful actions and yet they are still not willing to turn and run the other way forever.

They can express their shame, yet something still resists a final relinquishment of their body, mind, soul, and spirit. They adamantly refuse what others see as their escape route or their freedom train because it requires giving up control and surrendering. The thought of surrendering is paralyzing if there is no bigger picture or higher purpose.

In fact, in most recovery programs, the first three steps toward permanent transformation include *letting go* of the control of your life, *admitting* that your life is uncontrollable, and then *giving control* of your life over to God. (Here is the "God thing" again, as my walking buddy Jane calls it.)

Very often, these three steps themselves become stumbling blocks!

Surrendering, turning over control, is just too uncertain.

From the observer's perspective, you want so badly to say to the addict, "Can't you see that you *are* surrendering to something? You are giving over control of your life to a substance that destroys you, but you fear that something more demeaning, sinister, or embarrassing will occur if you give over control of your life to God who loves you? Can you not see that your life is completely in the tank right now, a mess, embarrassing, hopeless? How would asking God for help pose a greater threat to your sanity, sobriety, or happiness?"

Perhaps this is it. Surrender, indeed, is a point of no return. It is final.

But isn't that what you are looking for? Permanent transformation? Lasting change?

FROM TEMPORAL TO ETERNAL

When I first met Roger, he was the executive director of a youth program in Cleveland, Ohio, in which I was a volunteer.

From the moment we met, we shared a passion for helping students.

During that first year, Roger was influential in identifying my love for people, my gift of gab, and my passion to *change* lives. After only a few months, Roger encouraged me to intern with the organization, and I went on staff. We worked together with the same purpose and passion. We fell in love and got married.

We worked endless hours, as all workers in the helping profession tend to do, especially those who work with kids. And after long nights at bowling alleys, on retreats, and in a caravan of buses with up to two hundred high school kids after spending all day at an amusement park, Rog would gently remind our band of forty volunteers and staff, "Your reward is in heaven."

We'd all think, *Are you sure? It better be . . . 'cause we're tired!*

With students, you always have to understand that they may never return the time, energy, love, and friendship you invest in their lives. You may never see these kids again; they rarely return and say thanks. They usually eat all your food and will talk for hours on the phone about a date night that will be forgotten within a month! They live in the *now*!

Roger's job was to always remind us that what we did now would make a difference in their futures. He gave us eternal perspective.

Eventually we had a son, and our lives became even busier. We moved to California and continued helping people, both starting our own endeavors, his a nonprofit counseling-based organization, and mine a multimedia company designed to change lives through resources, events, television, and radio.

In 2000, we eventually found a peaceful little parcel that fulfilled the term *dream home.*

Three years have passed, and our home is our one haven of rest in a world full of unrest. It is the place where we celebrated our twenty-fifth wedding anniversary with family and friends and where we regularly enjoy beautiful sunsets. Comfy, casual, quiet . . . we love it.

But EVERY MORNING THAT I AWAKE, I HAVE A SENSE OF DESTINY, OF UNFINISHED BUSINESS. There is a nagging thought that I have been put on this earth to do something. Something more.

I also know that I have not accomplished it yet.

There is within me something unfulfilled, incomplete.

I'm still on the journey to take the life-changing message of Change Your Life to daily television and radio. As I write this, I have not yet found a producer or network to produce the *Change Your Life* TV® show, or help me launch the *Change Your Life Daily* radio show.

I've been to New York and Los Angeles at least fifteen (maybe even more) times since 1998, pounding the pavement and meeting with people with little tangible result, yet I will not give up on my dream to change people's lives for the better.

And even though I have faced plenty of "no, not now" responses, I keep knocking on doors, sending proposals, and meeting with people who will listen to my idea. And still . . . no open door.

So I sat down with my husband last month and asked him if we could sell the dream home in order to launch the dream.

We thought about it for many days and came to the same conclusion: What do you gain if you own a house with a view and do not fulfill your calling in life?

We began the process. We met with a realtor and are looking at other locations to call home. We don't know what turn of events might take place, even before the publishing of this book, but we can leave the view behind to live for something more, something eternal.

FROM SHAME TO SACRIFICE

In a book I wrote more than thirteen years ago, I told a remarkable story about my friend Kinney. It began with the heartache of a couple who had tried for many years but could not have a baby. I happened to be at a conference with my friend Kinney where she and a perfect stranger met and spoke.

The result of the conversation sparked a series of events that culminated in an adoption connection only six weeks later. The story of the woman who finally brought a baby home to be hers has always inspired those who have read or heard it. Now, that "baby," Ginny, is about to graduate from high school. Here is Ginny's story, as told from *her* perspective . . .

> She thought she was in love. He was in college; she was a junior in high school. By the time she returned to school in August for her senior year, her whole world had drastically changed. She was six months pregnant. She knew she could not raise a baby, not now. She

still had her entire life ahead of her. She was confused, but she wanted to do the right thing. It was hard, facing schoolmates, teachers, and people in her community where judgmental eyes fell on her everywhere she went. There seemed to be no solution that brought her peace.

Many childless couples expressed an interest in adopting her baby, but she continued to feel restless and unsure of what to do. Suddenly she was accountable for the life of another human being—a responsibility no teenage girl is ready for.

By November, she still had not made a solid decision, and the baby was due in weeks. Yet one couple caught her attention, and when she read a personal letter from the woman, she finally decided that her baby belonged with these two people.

The baby was born December 8 and went home with her loving new parents thirteen days later. This young woman's decision to give her baby life, despite the tremendous hardships she and the father faced themselves in doing so, is the only reason I am able today to express my gratitude, admiration, and love for the woman who brought me into this world.

Eighteen years ago, the two people who brought me into this world were brave enough to take responsibility for their actions and find the best way they could to right the situation for everyone's sake, including their unborn baby's.

School pressures, social expectations, and just life itself are hard enough to deal with during the teenage years. Can you imagine what it would be like to find yourself pregnant? It would turn your life upside down, to say the least. First think of the social aspects: how shameful it must feel to have everyone know your situation. You could even be asked to leave your school.

Then picture yourself over the nine months of pregnancy. How unbearable it must be at times, completely overwhelming for a teen. Remember the father as well; what the relationship must be like now, when, no matter how unintentionally, together you have created a new life. There is no option that is truly an easy way out.

The day I meet my birth parents is one I look forward to with more anticipation every day. The decisions they were obligated to make at such a young and tumultuous time in their lives affected the very life of another. Especially in the last few years have I realized what a great sacrifice it was for my birth mother to carry me for nine months, knowing that as soon as all the suffering was over she would have to give me up. Yet my birth parents looked beyond their own traumatic circumstances and chose to give me life. For that, no matter where they have been or where they are right now in this world, they will always be heroes to me.

Ginny, now a young woman at the same age her mother was when she gave her up for adoption, sees her birth mother, not as shameful, but as one who made an incredible sacrifice of love.

FROM PROMISES MADE TO PROMISES KEPT

Recently my girlfriend and I attended a wedding together. Until it began, we chatted festively with others before taking our seats. We had both been to many weddings, so we knew what to expect. First would come the lovely bridal procession, then the familiar vows.

It was at that moment the vows were spoken that my friend began to weep softly. She said, "A bride her age has no idea that those words could ever become reality in her life."

At thirty-two, my girlfriend is a recent widow. She was married only two years when her husband was diagnosed with terminal cancer. A career woman on a very direct path to success, she abruptly quit her job on the very day of her husband's diagnosis. In fact, it was on that day—in a hospital room—that I met her.

From day one, I watched in awe as this young bride fulfilled her marriage vows. Without skipping a beat, she became a fully committed on-line or on-the-phone medical researcher and an at-home nurse, chauffeur, and full-time specialty cook. I rarely heard her complain—and I spoke with her almost daily during the fourteen months of her husband's illness.

Until the day he died she was committed to her husband, even though he was physically and emotionally a different man than the one she had married two years earlier. Even up until the hour he died, she was very much in love with him, not willing to give up the fight, still hoping and praying for a miracle.

What was most remarkable during this long battle was that she did not struggle to keep her vows to love and cherish her husband until death parted them. She was unwavering in her commitment toward him. She was patient, loving, nurturing, and selfless.

Her promise to love him was fiercely tested. When others might have buckled under the pressure, her vows were pillars that held her up in the most terrifying situations. L O V E GAVE HER PERSPECTIVE WHEN ALL ELSE GAVE HER REASON TO RUN.

Not until she attended that wedding as a widow did she ever consider how deeply her words would be tested when she was a bride. By standing firm on her promises during her darkest moments, neither fear nor disappointment could overtake her.

As she remained true to her words, they gave her the courage to proceed. Her vows powerfully defined the beginning, middle, and final days of her marriage.

FROM DESIRING CHANGE TO KEEPING THE CHANGE

For more than twenty-six years, almost *every* time I speak to an audience and in every book I've written, I've told the story about the janitor named Ralph who found me wandering around a church, near the janitor's closet, on August 26, 1976.

I had absolutely no idea what I was doing at a church because I was neither religious nor holy, but I *was* suicidal and completely desperate with nowhere else to turn.

After only a few minutes of hearing my tearful confession—a drunk who might be pregnant by one of two men, who had just been in court for driving while intoxicated, and who was addicted to drugs—Ralph told me that God loved me just the way I was. Then he led me in a simple prayer. By the time I opened my eyes I saw life completely differently. And within hours, I *lived* life completely differently, much to the astonishment of everyone who knew me. Love had changed my life.

I was peaceful instead of suicidal.

I was sober instead of always drunk.

I lived by faith, not by fear.

I felt respect instead of shame.

And love has helped me keep the change.

In the summer of 2001, while interviewing me on a nationally syndicated radio show called *Focus on the Family*, the host, Dr. James Dobson, spontaneously asked me if I had kept in touch with Ralph, the janitor.

I was taken by surprise and said, "No. Actually, I lost track of Ralph only three months after I met him. The last thing I told Ralph was that I was going to return to Cleveland to show and tell my parents about my changed life, and he said he was going to live in Israel."

Within an hour after this radio show aired in more than two hundred U.S. cities, my office received a call from a woman whose brother's name was Ralph, who used to be a janitor of a church in northern California in 1976, and who currently lived in Israel.

On August 26, 2001, twenty-five years to the day that my life radically changed, I got a call from Ralph in Israel. He not only remembered me, but I could tell him, *"I kept the change!"*

Never, Never Give Up

This week I received another rejection letter. I don't know what is worse—hearing it over the phone or reading it in a letter.

A friend's child recently received news that the scholarship the family was expecting is not coming due to circumstances beyond their control.

Another friend just called. His daughter was caught stealing money and abusing cocaine again. He thought the previous treatment center had worked.

I received an e-mail that detailed a friend's cancer update. She's back in the hospital, tubes everywhere. The direction and prognosis of the disease aren't going well.

A different friend caught her spouse with another woman. Their world is shattered . . . and the pieces are everywhere.

When all else fails—and believe me, you might find yourself at this place many times on the path toward permanent transformation—there is hope.

HOPE COMES THE MOMENT YOU DETERMINE THAT NEITHER SETBACKS NOR CRITICISM ARE ENOUGH TO STOP YOU.

Reaching for permanent change is a decision of your mind,

body, soul, and spirit to find another way. If you don't give up, you will have an overcoming story. You will leave a legacy.

Son of a Rabbi

Judah Folkman was the son of a rabbi. As a child, he went with his father to visit patients of his congregation who were in the hospital. After a year, Judah told his father, "I can do what you're doing much better if I'm a doctor." And from that time Judah had a passion for medicine.

In the 1940s, when the U.S. Navy drafted young doctors to help find a long-lasting substitute for whole blood, Dr. Judah Folkman was recruited. Through a series of experiments with hemoglobin, Folkman felt he had stumbled onto something, but he had no idea it would be thirty years before he would understand it to be the process by which tumors are able to recruit their own private blood supply.

In the 1970s, at a time when everyone else thought the secret to understanding cancer lay deep within the cancer cell, only Judah Folkman was looking at blood vessels. Starving cancer by cutting off its food supply was his revolutionary idea, but it was met with incredible resistance by his peers. He speculated that if new blood-vessel growth to the tumor could be blocked, the tumor could not grow.

Judah Folkman was suggesting an entirely new way to treat cancer, but he faced swift and severe criticism. When he spoke at meetings, fellow researchers walked out. He had trouble getting published, and postdoctoral students were advised to stay away from him. He knew there was only one way to quiet his doubtful colleagues. He started devising experiments—using the most tedious processes in science—to prove that tumor *angiogenesis* was real.

After *ten years* of research, even Dr. Folkman was discouraged. But he refused to give up. And then, with a single molecule, he finally proved his theory. As soon as word spread of his discovery, his critics immediately turned into competitors!

In an interview on *Nova*, Folkman stated, "In research, there is a very fine line between persistence and obstinacy. YOU DO NOT KNOW WHETHER IF YOU'RE PERSISTENT A LITTLE WHILE LONGER YOU'LL MAKE IT, or whether you're just being obstinate. And of course, you can keep on going, stay with an idea too long; it's called pigheadedness."

Despite his groundbreaking discovery, Dr. Folkman was determined to make an even greater impact in the field of cancer research. His determination would not leave his thoughts. He continually imagined, searched, and considered every possibility for finding a cure for cancer.

His answer came while sitting in synagogue one day. A mystery that had confounded scientists for a century suddenly made sense to him. He rushed out and headed immediately to his lab, where he enlisted his students and colleagues to endure an endless series of experiments. *It took another decade*, but he succeeded in proving that his inspiration was more than theory.

HE HELD ON TO HOPE . . .

Dr. Judah Folkman's forty-year pursuit to find a cure for cancer is an incredible story of a courageous man who fought against rejection and discouragement—not with or by the encouragement of others or with the confidence that comes in small steps, but by holding on and not giving up.

Once a lonely warrior in the battle against cancer, his story—and life—are lessons in perseverance. He inspires us to not give up on a noble idea, though its outcome is not guaranteed.

Former U.S. Surgeon General C. Everett Koop said of Dr. Judah Folkman, "When the history of medicine is written, it will be a story of a tremendous impact that was, at the beginning, pooh-poohed by his colleagues, at the end, proven to be what he said it would be."

Folkman's story is an illustration of what it takes to never give up: a combination of courage, discipline, humility, and faith.

Though setbacks and disappointments are inevitable in . . .

- ▶ the pursuit of a lifelong dream,
- ▶ achieving a difficult victory,
- ▶ overcoming an illness,
- ▶ permanently changing any area of your life

. . . no matter how many times you arrive at a closed door or an impending obstacle, you have one last radical approach: Resolve simply to hold on and keep holding on . . . one more day, one more hour, even one more minute.

Keep Your Eyes on the Prize

John Maxwell's book *Failing Forward* reads like a who's who of some of the most outstanding American politicians and businesspeople who, in spite of repeated failures, disapproving critics, and heartbreaking setbacks, were successful.

For example, did you know that R. H. Macy, the father of retail as we know it today, tried five different professions before he tried retail? And it wasn't even until his seventh attempt in retail that he opened his first Macy's store in 1858. In 1877 Macy died, yet his stores exist today all over America —and on into the twenty-first century—because he did not, would not, give up!

The common trait of the successful men and women described in Maxwell's book is tenacity; THEY SIMPLY REFUSED TO GIVE UP, LOSE COURAGE, OR LET GO OF THEIR DREAM. Had they given in to fear or doubt, quit after only a few attempts, accepted a crushing blow as a final defeat, or listened to those with more power who told them they could never achieve their goal, we would not have . . .

- ► researchers who discovered cures or vaccines,
- ► world record holders,
- ► discoveries and interventions such as electricity, airplanes, or motor vehicles.

These leaders encountered all these difficulties, yet they recognized they were not *defeated*. They started over again; they got back up after being knocked down because they knew that only those who refuse to give up have the opportunity to obtain the prize.

All these achievers believed they fought for an innovative, noble, helpful, or powerful cause. And in each case, it took all they had to give!

It required . . .

- ► more than one time,
- ► more than one idea,
- ► more than one phone call,
- ► more than one proposal,
- ► more than one experiment,
- ► more than one method.

Giving up was not an option for them. Giving up cannot be an option for you.

Every overcomer, achiever, and visionary will experience disappointment. All of them will be rejected in one way or another. They will risk and lose. They will have setbacks. They will attempt and fail. They will have to endure the pain, even bear the shame of short-term loss by never losing sight of the long-term goal.

No matter where you have been, what you have done, how overwhelming your goals or where you find yourself today . . . right now, YOU CAN REIGNITE A FIRE OF HOPE WITHIN YOURSELF BY MAKING ONE STATEMENT OF RESOLVE: "I WILL NOT GIVE UP *TODAY*." This is the best-told secret of great overcomers: *one day at a time*.

You may not see a way out or up this minute. But there *is* a way. You may not know—this hour—which is the right step to take or how long it will be before you find it, but if you refuse to give up, *that in itself* is a statement of your resolve that will give you hope to keep holding on.

Even when or if there is every reason to do so, if you *won't* give up, you will one day look back and add up the change.

A Radical Challenge

As I sit in my hotel room writing this final chapter, I am thrilled that my room overlooks Central Park. But when you are typing on a computer, you rarely look up from the screen. When I finally decided to peek at the view, my eye first caught a little white sign made by the hotel management. It was placed right next to the telephone, so I couldn't miss it.

It says, "Tell us the truth, the whole truth, and nothing but the truth." I took it as a little sign for me to tell you the truth one more time, in case you missed it!

The following lies almost killed me:

I believed the lie that I was worthless and unlovable.

I believed the lie that I could *never* change my lifestyle.

And so at twenty-one, I decided to commit suicide.

Just in time, I was told a simple truth.

I was told that God loved me just the way I was . . .

I knew no one else did or could, and in a split second . . .

I decided to believe the truth.

Within hours, all the desires to engage in destructive behavior died, but I didn't.

I began to live a radically changed, permanently transformed life.

And I've lived to tell the truth. **Live the life you desire. And tell others the whole truth about it.**

On the journey to keep change in my life, I have found a purpose for so much of my pain. As a result, I am compelled to encourage those who also believe lies about their bodies, relationships, and dreams. One of the greatest privileges of my life is meeting countless new friends who are also progressing toward permanent transformation. **Find a purpose in your pain and make a difference.**

One of the most helpful discoveries I have made along the way to lasting change has been a greater understanding of the personality traits. When I could clearly see how every person had his or her own unique blend of temperaments, I could more easily make allowances for my own and others' weaknesses while at the same time knowing how to tap into strengths. **Go after your goals with the full knowledge of your personality strengths.**

Over the years, many battles have been waged in my mind to take me back to old ways and bad habits. For me to hold on to change, I have had to remain focused on the goal, refusing to be swayed or distracted or discouraged by negative thinking. Most importantly, I have had to jealously guard my mind and carefully choose what images and thoughts I allow to enter it. Now that I look back, I realize that my earliest victories, where I overcame negative and self-destructive thought patterns as an addict, were just the training ground for me as a visionary. **Jealously guard what goes into your mind.**

Perhaps the place where I stalled most frequently in my progress toward permanent change was in the area of discipline. Though I recycled bad habits many times before getting to the place where my actions reflected my desires, when I was finally able to change my stubborn self by setting limits and drawing lines for my behaviors, I experienced true freedom. And only when my behavior changed did I begin to see progress. When new habits became a part of my daily lifestyle, only after time did I see permanent transformation. **Do not hesitate to set limits and draw lines. Though you must give up some territory, through a defined strategy you can achieve lasting change.**

The most life-changing daily exercise to which I subscribe is the activity of journaling. For me, journaling is a written record of . . .

- ► the lies and the truth,
- ► the purpose in my pain,
- ► the taming of my personality,
- ► the status of my mind battles,
- ► the ongoing development of my strategy for holding on to change,
- ► the day's struggles, achievements, prayers, and

➤ the perspective that fuels me to never, ever give up.

Capturing my daily reality is the ammunition I have needed to change my life for good. **How you choose to capture your daily reality is up to you. But be aware that it is both a non-negotiable and time-consuming component of this radical approach to permanent transformation.**

Holding on to perspective allows me to . . .

➤ fight for what is right,

➤ love unconditionally,

➤ bear the intolerable, and

➤ let go of the visible for the invisible.

Hold on to love at all times. Sometimes it will be the only perspective that allows you to keep the change.

I am the first to tell you that it will take enormous energy to . . .

➤ wait,

➤ hang on,

➤ persevere,

➤ hope,

➤ be positive, and

➤ refuse to give up.

I agree that it is *much* easier to quit and become complacent, pessimistic, defiant, or paralyzed than it is to fight for and keep the change.

Yet I am compelled to encourage you.

If you are at the end, if you have great fears, if you have been deeply hurt, if your life has spun out of control . . . you must not give up. If you are a struggler, a dreamer, or an achiever who needs help, get it! Build around yourself a team of support and encouragement. Daily go after the changes you desire so deeply. **And simply never, never give up.**

In the beginning of this book I promised that at the end I would issue you one final challenge. Here it is:

Take the time to write or e-mail me your responses to the following questions. In so doing, I believe you will be making the decision to wholeheartedly embrace permanent transformation . . .

What truth must *you* tell? _____

_____

_____

_____

_____

_____

What purpose have *you* discovered behind your pain?

_____

_____

_____

_____

_____

_____

Which of *your* personality strengths can help you keep the changes you deeply desire? _____

_____

_____

_____

_____

_____

_____

How must *you* jealously guard *your* mind—today and every day? _____

_____

_____

_____

_____

_____

_____

Define *your* strategy for permanently changing a specific area in *your* life . . . in writing (why, what, when, where, who, and how): _____

_____

_____

_____

_____

_____

Describe a daily journal method that you will incorporate into *your* life—beginning today (system, time of day, amount of time). _____

_____

_____

_____

_____

_____

Identify at least one powerful, new perspective in *your* life that *you* must embrace in order to experience lasting change.

_____

_____

_____

_____

_____

_____

_____

What dream, goal, or struggle will *you* never give up?

_____

_____

_____

_____

_____

_____

Keep the Change

If you embrace this radical approach, I sincerely believe that *you* can and will keep the change in your life—daily and forever.

Be encouraged,
Becky
letters@beckytirabassi.com

Your Personality Profile*

In each of the following rows of four words across, place an X in front of the one or two words that most often apply to you. Continue through all forty lines. If you are not sure which word most applies, use the strength and weakness word definitions on pages 187-194, or ask a spouse or a friend, or think of what your answer would have been when you were a child. When you have finished, compile your Xs on the Personality Profile Scoring Sheet on pages 195-196, where you will also find further instructions on how to determine your personality type.

STRENGTHS

1 ___Adventurous	___Adaptable	___Animated	___Analytical
2 ___Persistent	___Playful	___Persuasive	___Peaceful
3 ___Submissive	___Self-sacrificing	___Sociable	___Strong-willed
4 ___Considerate	___Controlled	___Competitive	___Convincing
5 ___Refreshing	___Respectful	___Reserved	___Resourceful
6 ___Satisfied	___Sensitive	___Self-reliant	___Spirited
7 ___Planner	___Patient	___Positive	___Promoter
8 ___Sure	___Spontaneous	___Scheduled	___Shy
9 ___Orderly	___Obliging	___Outspoken	___Optimistic
10 ___Friendly	___Faithful	___Funny	___Forceful
11 ___Daring	___Delightful	___Diplomatic	___Detailed
12 ___Cheerful	___Consistent	___Cultured	___Confident
13 ___Idealistic	___Independent	___Inoffensive	___Inspiring
14 ___Demonstrative	___Decisive	___Dry humor	___Deep
15 ___Mediator	___Musical	___Mover	___Mixes easily

* Adapted from the Personality Profile, created by Fred Littauer. Reprinted from *After Every Wedding Comes a Marriage* by Florence Littauer. Copyright © 1981, Harvest House Publishers. Used by permission. Not to be duplicated. Copies may be ordered by calling 800-433-6633 or visiting www.thepersonalities.com.

16	___Thoughtful	___Tenacious	___Talker	___Tolerant
17	___Listener	___Loyal	___Leader	___Lively
18	___Contented	___Chief	___Chartmaker	___Cute
19	___Perfectionist	___Pleasant	___Productive	___Popular
20	___Bouncy	___Bold	___Behaved	___Balanced

WEAKNESSES

21	___Blank	___Bashful	___Brassy	___Bossy
22	___Undisciplined	___Unsympathetic	___Unenthusiastic	___Unforgiving
23	___Reticent	___Resentful	___Resistant	___Repetitious
24	___Fussy	___Fearful	___Forgetful	___Frank
25	___Impatient	___Insecure	___Indecisive	___Interrupts
26	___Unpopular	___Uninvolved	___Unpredictable	___Unaffectionate
27	___Headstrong	___Haphazard	___Hard to please	___Hesitant
28	___Plain	___Pessimistic	___Proud	___Permissive
29	___Angered easily	___Aimless	___Argumentative	___Alienated
30	___Naive	___Negative attitude	___Nervy	___Nonchalant
31	___Worrier	___Withdrawn	___Workaholic	___Wants credit
32	___Too sensitive	___Tactless	___Timid	___Talkative
33	___Doubtful	___Disorganized	___Domineering	___Depressed
34	___Inconsistent	___Introvert	___Intolerant	___Indifferent
35	___Messy	___Moody	___Mumbles	___Manipulative
36	___Slow	___Stubborn	___Show-off	___Skeptical
37	___Loner	___Lord over others	___Lazy	___Loud
38	___Sluggish	___Suspicious	___Short-tempered	___Scatterbrained
39	___Revengeful	___Restless	___Reluctant	___Rash
40	___Compromising	___Critical	___Crafty	___Changeable

STRENGTH DEFINITIONS

1

Adventurous. One who will take on new and daring enterprises with a determination to master them.

Adaptable. Easily fits and is comfortable in any situation.

Animated. Full of life, lively use of hand, arm, and face gestures.

Analytical. Likes to examine the parts for their logical and proper relationships.

2

Persistent. Sees one project through to its completion before starting another.

Playful. Full of fun and good humor.

Persuasive. Convinces through logic and fact rather than charm or power.

Peaceful. Seems undisturbed and tranquil and retreats from any form of strife.

3

Submissive. Easily accepts any other's point of view or desire with little need to assert his own opinion.

Self-sacrificing. Willingly gives up his own personal being for the sake of, or to meet the needs of others.

Sociable. One who sees being with others as an opportunity to be cute and entertaining rather than as a challenge or business opportunity.

Strong-willed. Determined to have one's own way.

4

Considerate. Having regard for the needs and feelings of others.

Controlled. Has emotional feelings but rarely displays them.

Competitive. Turns every situation, happening, or game into a contest and always plays to win!

Convincing. Can win you over to anything through the sheer charm of his personality.

5

Refreshing. Renews and stimulates or makes others feel good.

Respectful. Treats others with deference, honor, and esteem.

Reserved. Self-restrained in expression of emotion or enthusiasm.

Resourceful. Able to act quickly and effectively in virtually all situations.

6

Satisfied. A person who easily accepts any circumstance or situation.

Sensitive. Intensively cares about others, and what happens.

Self-reliant. An independent person who can fully rely on his own capabilities, judgment, and resources.

Spirited. Full of life and excitement.

7

Planner. Prefers to work out a detailed arrangement beforehand, for the accomplishment of project or goal, and prefers involvement with the planning stages and the finished product rather than the carrying out of the task.

Patient. Unmoved by delay, remains calm and tolerant.

Positive. Knows it will turn out right if he's in charge.

Promoter. Urges or compels others to go along, join, or invest through the charm of his own personality.

8

Sure. Confident, rarely hesitates or wavers.

Spontaneous. Prefers all of life to be impulsive, unpremeditated activity, not restricted by plans.

Scheduled. Makes, and lives, according to a daily plan, dislikes his plan to be interrupted.

Shy. Quiet, doesn't easily instigate a conversation.

9

Orderly. Having a methodical, systematic arrangement of things.

Obliging. Accommodating. One who is quick to do it another's way.

Outspoken. Speaks frankly and without reserve.

Optimistic. Sunny disposition who convinces self and others that everything will turn out all right.

10

Friendly. A responder rather than an initiator, seldom starts a conversation.

Faithful. Consistently reliable, steadfast, loyal, and devoted sometimes beyond reason.

Funny. Sparkling sense of humor that can make virtually any story into an hilarious event.

Forceful. A commanding personality whom others would hesitate to take a stand against.

11

Daring. Willing to take risks; fearless, bold.

Delightful. A person who is upbeat and fun to be with.

Diplomatic. Deals with people tactfully, sensitively, and patiently.

Detailed. Does everything in proper order with a clear memory of all the things that happen.

12

Cheerful. Consistently in good spirits and promoting happiness in others.

Consistent. Stays emotionally on an even keel, responding as one might expect.

Cultured. One whose interests involve both intellectual and artistic pursuits, such as theatre, symphony, ballet.

Confident. Self-assured and certain of own ability and success.

13

Idealistic. Visualizes things in their perfect form, and has a need to measure up to that standard himself.

Independent. Self-sufficient, self-supporting, self-confident and seems to have little need of help.

Inoffensive. A person who never says or causes anything unpleasant or objectionable.

Inspiring. Encourages others to work, join, or be involved, and makes the whole thing fun.

14

Demonstrative. Openly expresses emotion, especially affection, and doesn't hesitate to touch others while speaking to them.

Decisive. A person with quick, conclusive, judgment-making ability.

Dry humor. Exhibits "dry wit," usually one-liners which can be sarcastic in nature.

Deep. Intense and often introspective with a distaste for surface conversation and pursuits.

15

Mediator. Consistently finds him- or herself in the role of reconciling differences in order to avoid conflict.

Musical. Participates in or has a deep appreciation for music, is committed to music as an art form, rather than the fun of performance.

Mover. Driven by a need to be productive, is a leader whom others follow, finds it difficult to sit still.

Mixes easily. Loves a party and can't wait to meet everyone in the room, never meets a stranger.

16

Thoughtful. A considerate person who remembers special occasions and is quick to make a kind gesture.

Tenacious. Holds on firmly, stubbornly, and won't let go until the goal is accomplished.

Talker. Constantly talking, generally telling funny stories and entertaining everyone around, feeling the need to fill the silence in order to make others comfortable.

Tolerant. Easily accepts the thoughts and ways of others without the need to disagree with or change them.

17

Listener. Always seems willing to hear what you have to say.

Loyal. Faithful to a person, ideal, or job, sometimes beyond reason.

Leader. A natural born director, who is driven to be in charge, and often finds it difficult to believe that anyone else can do the job as well.

Lively. Full of life, vigorous, energetic.

18

Contented. Easily satisfied with what he has, rarely envious.

Chief. Commands leadership and expects people to follow.

Chartmaker. Organizes life, tasks, and problem solving by making lists, forms or graphs.

Cute. Precious, adorable, center of attention.

19

Perfectionist. Places high standards on himself, and often on others, desiring that everything be in proper order at all times.

Pleasant. Easygoing, easy to be around, easy to talk with.

Productive. Must constantly be working or achieving, often finds it very difficult to rest.

Popular. Life of the party and therefore much desired as a party guest.

20

Bouncy. A bubbly, lively personality, full of energy.

Bold. Fearless, daring, forward, unafraid of risk.

Behaved. Consistently desires to conduct himself within the realm of what he feels is proper.

Balanced. Stable, middle of the road personality, not subject to sharp highs or lows.

WEAKNESS DEFINITIONS

21

Blank. A person who shows little facial expression or emotion.

Bashful. Shrinks from getting attention, resulting from self-consciousness.

Brassy. Showy, flashy, comes on strong, too loud.

Bossy. Commanding, domineering, sometimes overbearing in adult relationships.

22

Undisciplined. A person whose lack of order permeates most every area of his life.

Unsympathetic. Finds it difficult to relate to the problems or hurts of others.

Unenthusiastic. Tends to not get excited, often feeling it won't work anyway.

Unforgiving. One who has difficulty forgiving or forgetting a hurt or injustice done to them, apt to hold on to a grudge.

23

Reticent. Unwilling or struggles against getting involved, especially when complex.

Resentful. Often holds ill feelings as a result of real or imagined offenses.

Resistant. Strives, works against, or hesitates to accept any other way but his own.

Repetitious. Retells stories and incidents to entertain you without realizing he has already told the story several times before, is constantly needing something to say.

24

Fussy. Insistent over petty matters or details, calling for a great attention to trivial details.

Fearful. Often experiences feelings of deep concern, apprehension, or anxiousness.

Forgetful. Lack of memory which is usually tied to a lack of discipline and not bothering to mentally record things that aren't fun.

Frank. Straightforward, outspoken, and doesn't mind telling you exactly what he thinks.

25

Impatient. A person who finds it difficult to endure irritation or wait for others.

Insecure. One who is apprehensive or lacks confidence.

Indecisive. The person who finds it difficult to make any decision at all. (Not the personality that labors long over each decision in order to make the perfect one.)

Interrupts. A person who is more of a talker than a listener, who starts speaking without even realizing someone else is already speaking.

26

Unpopular. A person whose intensity and demand for perfection can push others away.

Uninvolved. Has no desire to listen or become interested in clubs, groups, activities, or other people's lives.

Unpredictable. May be ecstatic one moment and down the next, or willing to help but then disappears, or promises to come but forgets to show up.

Unaffectionate. Finds it difficult to verbally or physically demonstrate tenderness openly.

27

Headstrong. Insists on having his own way.

Haphazard. Has no consistent way of doing things.

Hard to please. A person whose standards are set so high that it is difficult to ever satisfy them.

Hesitant. Slow to get moving and hard to get involved.

28

Plain. A middle-of-the-road personality without highs or lows and showing little, if any, emotion.

Pessimistic. While hoping for the best, this person generally sees the down side of a situation first.

Proud. One with great self-esteem who sees himself as always right and the best person for the job.

Permissive. Allows others (including children) to do as they please in order to keep from being disliked.

29

Angered easily. One who has a childlike flash-in-the-pan temper that expresses itself in tantrum style and is over and forgotten almost instantly.

Aimless. Not a goal-setter with little desire to be one.

Argumentative. Incites arguments generally because he is right no matter what the situation may be.

Alienated. Easily feels estranged from others, often because of insecurity or fear that others don't really enjoy his company.

30

Naive. Simple and child-like perspective, lacking sophistication or comprehension of what the deeper levels of life are really about.

Negative attitude. One whose attitude is seldom positive and is often able to see only the down or dark side of each situation.

Nervy. Full of confidence, fortitude, and sheer guts, often in a negative sense.

Nonchalant. Easy-going, unconcerned, indifferent.

31

Worrier. Consistently feels uncertain, troubled, or anxious.

Withdrawn. A person who pulls back to himself and needs a great deal of alone or isolation time.

Workaholic. An aggressive goal-setter who must be constantly productive and feels very guilty when resting, is not driven by a need for perfection or completion but by a need for accomplishment and reward.

Wants credit. Thrives on the credit or approval of others. As an entertainer this person feeds on the applause, laughter, and/or acceptance of an audience.

32

Too sensitive. Overly introspective and easily offended when misunderstood.

Tactless. Sometimes expresses himself in a somewhat offensive and inconsiderate way.

Timid. Shrinks from difficult situations.

Talkative. An entertaining, compulsive talker who finds it difficult to listen.

33

Doubtful. Characterized by uncertainty and lack of confidence that it will ever work out.

Disorganized. Lack of ability to ever get life in order.

Domineering. Compulsively takes control of situations and/or people, usually telling others what to do.

Depressed. A person who feels down much of the time.

34

Inconsistent. Erratic, contradictory, with actions and emotions not based on logic.

Introvert. A person whose thoughts and interest are directed inward, lives within himself.

Intolerant. Appears unable to withstand or accept another's attitudes, point of view, or way of doing things.

Indifferent. A person to whom most things don't matter one way or the other.

35

Messy. Living in a state of disorder, unable to find things.

Moody. Doesn't get very high emotionally, but easily slips into low lows, often when feeling unappreciated.

Mumbles. Will talk quietly under the breath when pushed, doesn't bother to speak clearly.

Manipulative. Influences or manages shrewdly or deviously for his own advantage, will get his way somehow.

36

Slow. Doesn't often act or think quickly, too much of a bother.

Stubborn. Determined to exert his or her own will, not easily persuaded, obstinate.

Show-off. Needs to be the center of attention, wants to be watched.

Skeptical. Disbelieving, questioning the motive behind the words.

37

Loner. Requires a lot of private time and tends to avoid other people.

Lord over. Doesn't hesitate to let you know that he is right or is in control.

Lazy. Evaluates work or activity in terms of how much energy it will take.

Loud. A person whose laugh or voice can be heard above others in the room.

38

Sluggish. Slow to get started, needs push to be motivated.

Suspicious. Tends to suspect or distrust others or ideas.

Short-tempered. Has a demanding impatience-based anger and a short fuse. Anger is expressed when others are not moving fast enough or have not completed what they have been asked to do.

Scatterbrained. Lacks the power of concentration or attention, flighty.

39

Revengeful. Knowingly or otherwise holds a grudge and punishes the offender, often by subtly withholding friendship or affection.

Restless. Likes constant new activity because it isn't fun to do the same things all the time.

Reluctant. Unwilling or struggles against getting involved.

Rash. May act hastily, without thinking things through, generally because of impatience.

40

Compromising. Will often relax his position, even when right, in order to avoid conflict.

Critical. Constantly evaluating and making judgments, frequently thinking or expressing negative reactions.

Crafty. Shrewd, one who can always find a way to get to the desired end.

Changeable. A child-like, short attention span that needs a lot of change and variety to keep from getting bored.

PERSONALITY PROFILE SCORING SHEET

Transfer all your Xs from the strengths and weaknesses lists on pages 185-186 to the corresponding words in the columns below. For example, if you checked Animated on the profile, check it here on the scoring sheet. (Note: The words are in a different order on the profile and the scoring sheet.) Add up your totals in each column, then continue transferring Xs onto the columns on page 196.

Once you've transferred all your Xs to the scoring sheet and added up your subtotals from both the strengths and weaknesses sections, you'll know your dominant personality type. You'll also know what combination of personality types you are. If, for example, your score is 35 in Powerful Choleric strengths and weaknesses, there's really little question; you're almost all Powerful Choleric. But if your score is, for example, 16 in Powerful Choleric, 14 in Perfect Melancholy, and 5 in each of the others, you're a Powerful Choleric with a strong Perfect Melancholy. The totals will also tell you your least dominant personality type.

STRENGTHS

	Popular Sanguine	Powerful Choleric	Perfect Melancholy	Peaceful Phlegmatic
1	Animated	Adventurous	Analytical	Adaptable
2	Playful	Persuasive	Persistent	Peaceful
3	Sociable	Strong-willed	Self-sacrificing	Submissive
4	Convincing	Competitive	Considerate	Controlled
5	Refreshing	Resourceful	Respectful	Reserved
6	Spirited	Self-reliant	Sensitive	Satisfied
7	Promoter	Positive	Planner	Patient
8	Spontaneous	Sure	Scheduled	Shy
9	Optimistic	Outspoken	Orderly	Obliging
10	Funny	Forceful	Faithful	Friendly
11	Delightful	Daring	Detailed	Diplomatic
12	Cheerful	Confident	Cultured	Consistent
13	Inspiring	Independent	Idealistic	Inoffensive
14	Demonstrative	Decisive	Deep	Dry humor
15	Mixes easily	Mover	Musical	Mediator
16	Talker	Tenacious	Thoughtful	Tolerant
17	Lively	Leader	Loyal	Listener
18	Cute	Chief	Chartmaker	Contented
19	Popular	Productive	Perfectionist	Pleasant
20	Bouncy	Bold	Behaved	Balanced
Subtotals	—	—	—	—

WEAKNESSES

	Popular Sanguine	Powerful Choleric	Perfect Melancholy	Peaceful Phlegmatic
21	Brassy	Bossy	Bashful	Blank
22	Undisciplined	Unsympathetic	Unforgiving	Unenthusiastic
23	Repetitious	Resistant	Resentful	Reticent
24	Forgetful	Frank	Fussy	Fearful
25	Interrupts	Impatient	Insecure	Indecisive
26	Unpredictable	Unaffectionate	Unpopular	Uninvolved
27	Haphazard	Headstrong	Hard to please	Hesitant
28	Permissive	Proud	Pessimistic	Plain
29	Angered easily	Argumentative	Alienated	Aimless
30	Naive	Nervy	Negative attitude	Nonchalant
31	Wants credit	Workaholic	Withdrawn	Worrier
32	Talkative	Tactless	Too sensitive	Timid
33	Disorganized	Domineering	Depressed	Doubtful
34	Inconsistent	Intolerant	Introvert	Indifferent
35	Messy	Manipulative	Moody	Mumbles
36	Show-off	Stubborn	Skeptical	Slow
37	Loud	Lord over others	Loner	Lazy
38	Scatterbrained	Short-tempered	Suspicious	Sluggish
39	Restless	Rash	Revengeful	Reluctant
40	Changeable	Crafty	Critical	Compromising

Subtotals — — — —

Subtotals
from
page 195 — — — —

Grand
Totals — — — —

196

SAMPLE PAGES FROM

Change Your Life Daily Journal

The *Change Your Life Daily Journal*[*] is a four-page-a-day, twenty-minute journal exercise with a balanced-life approach to help you keep the change in your life physically, emotionally, spiritually, and mentally.

On each page, you are asked to make two journal entries that . . .

- ► express your plans and intentions to change,
- ► move you forward in daily steps, and
- ► provide you with a written record of your progress.

In essence, by making—and *keeping*—a daily appointment with yourself in writing, you are taking a powerful and positive step toward fulfilling your dreams, overcoming your struggles, and reaching your goals.

If you find these sample pages from the *Change Your Life Daily Journal* helpful, you can order the spiral-bound book from www.beckytirabassi.com.

[*]Becky Tirabassi, *Change Your Life Daily Journal* (Newport Beach, Calif.: BTCYL, Inc.: 1998)

date _____

e
m
o
t
i
o
n
a
l

forgive

To experience emotional balance on a daily basis, allow one or more of the questions below to prompt you to journal about the relationships in your life that need to heal and be healed.

Today, I know I need to ask _____ **to forgive me.**

I need to forgive myself for _____

I need to forgive _____ **for** _____

And I ask God to forgive me for _____

_____

_____

_____

_____

_____

_____

What additional step(s) can I take to complete the healing that I have just journaled about in the above space? (ex: a phone call, letter, apology,etc.)

_____

_____

_____

_____

give

The gift of time, money, resources, or talent to an organization or person is both a powerful and practical way to help others. **What need comes to my mind—today—that I can find and fill and/or what person or organization needs a specific source of comfort or encouragement that I can give?**

_____

_____

_____

_____

_____

change
your
life
daily _____

date _____

eat right

- · understand your own body type, genetics, metabolism, etc.
- · design a healthy, "plan ahead" eating plan that includes a balance of all the food groups in moderate portions
- · **record your daily intentions for meals and snacks below**
- · **review your progress and make daily adjustments**

breakfast	
lunch	
dinner	
snacks	

p
h
y
s
i
c
a
l

exercise regularly

- · determine what type of activity, where, when, how often, and with whom you most like to exercise
- · develop a "week at a glance" exercise plan that includes a variety of three to four activities and has provision for alternate dates and times

Detail your week plan; highlight today's plan . . . what? when? where? with whom?

sun	mon	tue	wed	thur	fri	sat

journal

Journal below about any temptations, circumstances or emotions—today— that might keep you from reaching your goals. (ex: vacation, celebrations, etc)

_____

_____

_____

_____

_____

_____

change
your
life
daily

date _____

m
e
n
t
a
l

detail your day

appointments

- *quiet time* ☐
- *work out* ☐
- _____ ☐
- _____ ☐
- _____ ☐
- _____ ☐
- _____ ☐
- _____ ☐
- _____ ☐
- _____ ☐
- _____ ☐
- _____ ☐
- _____ ☐
- _____ ☐
- _____ ☐
- _____ ☐
- _____

calls to make   *phone #*

_____

_____

_____

_____

_____

_____

letters to write/fax/email
                                  w   f   e
_____ ☐ ☐ ☐

_____ ☐ ☐ ☐

_____ ☐ ☐ ☐

_____ ☐ ☐ ☐

things to do

_____ ☐

_____ ☐

_____ ☐

_____ ☐

_____ ☐

define your dream

What is one practical step you can take toward reaching a goal—and fulfilling a dream—in one or more areas of your life?

Use this space to brainstorm or to develop a dream that won't go away!

physical | emotional
mental | spiritual

change
your
life
daily

date _____

talk to God

Today, in honest transparency, share—in writing—your thoughts,
gratitude, regrets, fears, plans, hopes, dreams and requests
for yourself and others with the living, loving God.

s
p
i
r
i
t
u
a
l

_____

_____

_____

_____

_____

_____

_____

_____

_____

_____

_____

_____

_____

_____

_____

_____

_____

_____

listen to God

God's voice is found in His Word, the Bible.
Unless you have another system, read today's **change your life Daily Bible** using
today's date. Write in this area any verse or verses that stand out, touch your heart,
encourage or correct you. **What is God saying to you today?**

_____

_____

_____

_____

_____

_____

change
your
life
daily